Spirit in the Cities

Spirit in the Cities

Searching for Soul in the Urban Landscape

Kathryn Tanner, editor

Fortress Press/Minneapolis

SPIRIT IN THE CITIES
Copyright © 2004 Augsburg Fortress. All rights reserved. Except for brief quotations in critical articles or reviews, no part of this book may be reproduced in any manner without prior written permission from the publisher. Write: Permissions, Augsburg Fortress, Box 1209, Minneapolis, MN 55440.

Cover art: *Somewhere in Berkeley* (1989) by Gregory Blake Larson (b.1961, American). Oil on canvas. ©Private Collection/Greg Larson/SuperStock. Used by permission.

Cover and book design: Zan Ceeley

Library of Congress Cataloging-in-Publication Data
Spirit in the cities : searching for soul in the urban landscape / Kathryn Tanner, editor.
    p. cm.
Includes bibliographical references.
ISBN 0-8006-3682-1 (pbk : alk. paper)
    1. Cities and towns — Religious aspects — Christianity. 2. Theology, Doctrinal. I. Tanner, Kathryn.
    BR115.C45S68 2004
                                        2004011402

The paper used in this publication meets the minimum requirements of American National Standard for Information Sciences — Permanence of Paper for Printed Library Materials, ANSI Z329.48-1984.

Manufactured in the U.S.A.
08   07   06   05   04   1   2   3   4   5   6   7   8   9   10

Contents

About the Contributors

Sheila Briggs is an Associate Professor in the School of Religion at the University of Southern California. Among her current interests are slavery in early Christianity and religious and moral themes in cult television. She is co-editing a forthcoming handbook on feminist theology from Oxford University Press.

M. Shawn Copeland is Associate Professor of Theology at Boston College and President of the Catholic Theological Association of America. Her research interests include theological and philosophical anthropology, and political theology. The author of over sixty articles, book chapters, and edited books, she has lectured extensively in the U.S., Canada, Australia, Belgium, and Nigeria.

Ada María Isasi-Díaz was born and raised in La Habana, Cuba, and is Professor of Christian Ethics and Theology at Drew

University in Madison, New Jersey, and author of *En la Lucha: Elaborating a Mujerista Theology* (revised edition, Fortress Press 2004) and *La Lucha Continues—Mujerista Theology* (2004).

Linda Mercadante is B. Robert Straker Professor of Theology at the Methodist Theological School in Ohio. She holds her doctorate from Princeton Theological Seminary and is the author of *Victims & Sinners: Spiritual Roots of Addiction and Recovery* (1996) and *Gender, Doctrine, and God: The Shakers and Contemporary Theology* (1990).

Kathryn Tanner is Professor of Theology at the Divinity School, University of Chicago, and author of *The Politics of God: Christian Theologies and Social Justice* (1992), *Theories of Culture: A New Agenda for Theology* (1997), and *Jesus, Humanity, and the Trinity: A Brief Systematic Theology* (2001), all from Fortress Press.

Mark Lewis Taylor is Professor of Theology and Culture at Princeton Theological Seminary, editor of *Paul Tillich: Theologian of the Boundaries* (1987), and author of *Remembering Esperanza: A Cultural-Political Theology for North American Praxis* (1990; 2004), and *The Executed God: The Way of the Cross in Lockdown America* (2001), all from Fortress Press.

Preface
Kathryn Tanner

Cities are back. In our world of Internet connection and globalized economic exchange, one sign of the times is urban resurgence. Cities and towns as commercial centers and transportation hubs were once the heart of industrial capitalism but lost influence with the shift of population and production to the suburbs and the general deindustrialization of America. Now cities—with the technical infrastructure to support global economic transactions and with the service and entertainment sectors to support the high-flying lifestyles of the economic elite—are once again central.

Cities are the managerial nodes for the lightning-fast exchanges of international finance and for the complex coordination essential to the internal operations of multinational corporations. Low-paid workers from all over the world are drawn into this urban infrastructure for global capitalism and international finance, so that the city becomes a microcosm of the uneven development of capitalism worldwide. The privileged of the developed regions of the world and the economically oppressed of the less developed ones meet side by side in our cities.[1]

In this increasingly globalized, Internet-connected world, another sign of the times is, ironically, space. "We are in the epoch of simultaneity; we are in the epoch of juxtaposition . . . of the side by side, of the dispersed . . . . Our experience of the world is less that of a long life developing through time than that of a network that connects points and intersects with its own skein."[2] Our moment on the world historical stage is no longer commonly understood in terms of a present torn between past and future, between stasis and change—between conservative, backward-leaning forces bent on sustaining, unchanged, the achievements of the past, and forward-looking, future-oriented movements for progress. Instead, our time is being defined by our decisions about how persons, products, and processes are to circulate and be arranged in space. Fundamental political and economic questions concern the transnational movements of workers, shifting sites of production and consumption in a world dominated by multinational corporations, the connection or disconnection of regions to global financial and media networks, and the way bodies—whether they be in prisons or ghettoes, or on factory floors—are corralled and enclosed, measured and manipulated. "Prophecy now involves a geographical rather than historical projection" once one realizes "that it is now space more than time that hides things from us, that the demystification of spatiality and its veiled instrumentality of power is the key to making practical, political, and theoretical sense of the contemporary era."[3]

Space from this new point of view is no longer the passive, already given, empty container through which historical processes flow. History is instead found materialized in varying spatial arrangements; history becomes a matter of how space comes to be organized. Space, in short, is now understood both as the product of social processes and as an influence upon them. Capitalism, for example, is not simply temporalizing—always revolutionizing the production process, dooming to obsolescence, and chasing the new. It is also a force for ever-new spatial configurations—pushing people out of their settled agrarian existences, concentrating populations and production sites, connecting disparate regions of the world (raw materials becoming inputs for far-off production; products then shipped away for consumption elsewhere), creating and feeding off of divisions between town and country, city and suburb, developed and underdeveloped regions of the world. As such a social product and social force, "space is not a scientific object removed from ideology and politics; it has always been political and strategic. . . . Space has been shaped and molded from historical and natural elements, but this has been a political process. Space is political and ideological. It is a product literally filled with ideologies."[4] Politics and ideology help configure space and are consequently embedded in the way space is arranged and the way people move through it. The social construction of space therefore calls for an interpretive geography—a hermeneutics of suspicion for space, if you will—that might uncover the history, power dynamics, and cultural biases materialized there.

The chapters in this volume take off from both these signs of the times, to offer spiritual cityscapes, religious views of urban places. They lay out the physical geographies of various urban sites— Los Angeles, Detroit, Newark, Philadelphia, Havana—in ways that combine theological and political discernment. Often, in a quite personal fashion, they narrate, among other things: the concrete shape of physical locations (a Newark neighborhood; an automobile assembly line in Detroit); the way different areas of a city like Los Angeles both connect and disjoin to form a complex patchwork visible to train and bus riders but invisible from the freeway; the competing processions of tourists and protest marchers in Philadelphia; the movements of displaced persons circulating back to and then away again from places they still consider home. In the process, each author makes clear how we are constituted by social spaces, by the quite physical layout of the places we inhabit and pass through.

Political discernment, too, is a part of these tales. Each essay provides a sense for how things got arranged this way and for the sort of community or lack of it that such arrangements foster. Each uncovers the history and political stakes materialized in these places—quite concretely in their architecture, in the movements they encourage or forbid, and in what they reveal or hide from view. Theological discernment is also an integral part of these reflections in that each tries to track the forces for spiritual regeneration or degeneration, for life enhancement or disempowerment, contained in these places; each asks after the possible theological significance of their arrangement. Is this the sort of cityscape that might physically embody an incarnate God? Is this a place where grace can be concretely realized? Are these movements in space—between old and new homelands—a way to shape a liberating historical project?

In so doing, the authors rethink contextual theology in spatial terms. Contextual theology—theology that owns up to the influence of race, class, and gender, theology that self-consciously addresses problems endemic to those specific social locations—becomes a theology of quite physical geographical contexts: of architecture and transportation, of travel and emigration, of public processions and urban divisions. The usual matters of contextual theology are all found concretely embedded in these shifting sites, to be unpacked or unwound through combined political and religious analysis and critique.

Understood in this concrete physical fashion, contextual theology begins to reveal the ever-broadening nontraditional locations of religious questioning in our cities. This questioning often takes place out of sight of theology as it is commonly practiced in university and seminary settings; indeed, it takes place "off-site" with reference to either academy or church. How is one to make sense religiously of physical abandonment—of the deserted buildings and empty shops and all that they entail for people's external and internal well-being? Of the ordering of workplaces and of the damaged relations between workers and managers that such ordering embeds? Of the disconnections and divisions in our cities that alienate and blind us? Of those fundamental movements through life that essentially involve movements in space—the loss of one's original homeland, or guilt-ridden escapes from declining neighborhoods? Of the anger and shame of those forced to stay?

Moving as the spirit does, without regard for the usual boundaries of religious institutions, spirits of resistance surface in these nontraditional urban locations of religious questioning. Those spirits of resistance emerge in forces for humanization and regeneration. They can be found in new communities that enable people to cope, survive, and hope within and across the multiple urban locations. Resources for life and healing well up through the interstices of city life, as these authors envisage and re-envisage cityscapes through a religious lens. People are centered and reconnected in ways that make the ordinary seem extraordinary, in ways that offer hope for some breakthrough to life-giving forces of support to those in need. Today's cities are religiously vibrant in new and exciting ways.

Loci theology—a theology organized according to settled topics—becomes in this way a theology of new, often overlooked, places. In an odd but deeply appropriate subversion of its usual connotation, the "loci" of loci theology—from the Latin *locus* meaning place—shifts its meaning from commonplaces of theological discussion to, literally, unexpected places. But the contents of the traditional theological themes of loci theology are also altered, accordingly, to highlight their spatial forms. Sin, grace, spiritual renewal, transcendence, incarnation, reconciliation, and liberative redemption are all fundamentally reconfigured spatially to suit the problematics of an urban geography. At issue are mobility and rootedness in place, dislocation and belonging, connection and disjunction, occlusion and display, division and incorporation, exclusion and inclusion—new, redemptive orderings of all these spatial forms so as to rework the old in life-enhancing and spiritually fulfilling ways.

The authors are all members of the Workgroup on Constructive Theology, which got its start in the mid-1970s as a forum to encourage collaborative and constructive (rather than merely methodologically preoccupied) work in academic theology with attention to new shifts in the field and new problems of the times. As chair of the Workgroup between 1992 and 1998, I oversaw a series of meetings in Newark and Chicago in which we tried to

enter into conversation with individuals and communities struggling to improve the lives of people in these urban areas, in order to
engage the implicit or explicit theologies emerging there. Without
much of a formal prior agenda, we simply wanted to learn from
others about the problems with which they struggled, and to reflect
with them about how religious questions or institutions entered
into their own hopes for change. In Newark we met with cloistered
Dominican nuns, AIDS caregivers from the Episcopal church, prac-
titioners of Santería and candomblé, black leaders of mainline
churches, and members of an ecumenical Islamic cultural center. In
Chicago we visited with staff of the Night Ministry (an organization
that tries to "build relationships with persons of the nighttime
streets that empower them to meet their needs") and some of us
accompanied them on their rounds; we also had spirited theological discussions with women currently or formerly involved in prostitution who were participating as clients or program organizers in
the residence and outreach programs of Genesis House. The general idea behind all this was to help ourselves, and the people we
met, to think theologically about crucial issues affecting people on
a daily basis in urban environments. Using the resources of our academic training in theology and our access to other academic disciplines such as economics, politics, and social theory, we hoped to
lift them up and reflect with them upon the theology already at
work in their daily lives as persons committed to social change, and
to bring the results of that reflection back to bear on the pressing
issues of urban life in ways that might aid such struggles for
change. Practicing this sort of engagement between academic theology and grassroots political theology together at our meetings,
Workgroup members would then go off and do the same sort of
thing more thoroughly and realistically for the communities of
struggle and the urban environments with which they were personally associated. The energy for this part of the group experiment
faded. But the process itself during that six-year period nevertheless
represented a significant rethinking of constructive and collaborative work—again, in spatial terms, in a spatially materialized form,
albeit an ephemeral one.

Constructive theological work during our time together was literally the construction of new spaces; the new spaces of interaction
that we created by venturing to different cities for theological
engagement with people working for change in those environments, the new spaces formed by bridging our usual locations as
academics with the religious forces afoot in the cities we visited.
Rather than amounting to the sharing of formal papers for the purpose of mutual criticism and the advancement of new ideas, our
collaboration became a more event-centered performance, enacted
in and through the construction of these new spaces of interaction.
Our collaboration was the active constitution of a group around the
shared experiences of our urban excursions to Newark and
Chicago. It occurred as we moved together into those urban spaces
to engage others; it occurred in our conversations with people in
those urban sites that we entered for a time and left behind. Our
dialogue partners, we hoped, received their own experiences back
from us with a difference informed by our competence as academic
theologians, but this collaboration with persons in urban locales
other than our own also surely affected our work as professional
theologians. These chapters—with their occasional odd mix of personal narrative, historical recounting, political analysis, and theological rumination—are some of the sedimented effects of what was
stirred up for a time in those new spaces of interaction. The won-
derfully unexpected precipitate is the shape-shifting theology on
display here—theology that flows across the usual divides between
intimate personal history and academic treatment of global social
forces, theology that opens up religious reflection to the concrete,
pluriform dimensions of life by embedding it in the physical details
of place while allowing religious reflection to move with the spirit,
toward the newly configured terrains of full human flourishing.

1

Taking the Train

A Theological Journey through
Contemporary Los Angeles County

Sheila Briggs

When I was on sabbatical in London in 1992 and 1993, I didn't have a car, which was fortunate since there is nowhere to park a car in central London. I was also overjoyed to be released from the daily compulsion to drive a car, which afflicts every resident of Southern California. I took the bus everywhere—much to the amusement of my wealthy host, who always used taxis, but to whom I pointed out that if she walked a couple of hundred yards from her home, she could take a bus literally to the door of her law offices. I went all over London on the bus, to the libraries of King's College, to the bookstores on Charing Cross Road. I became aware that these physical journeys were cultural and political ones as well. There were the obvious markers of Britain's colonial past and multicultural present—the West Africans, the Irish, the people from the Caribbean and the Indian subcontinent and the Britons of every conceivable ancestry and mixture of ancestry. But on the bus I was not only sitting next to people, I was traveling with them through an urban space in which all our lives were emplotted. When we talk about "social location," this has a very physical and concrete correlate. It is the space—the streets and buildings we pass—in which our identity is transacted in the social relations that we either engage in or refer to in that space. The postmodern sensibility holds that we each are constructed by multiple identities; this is physically enacted in the urban landscape of cities like London or Los Angeles. It can be seen in the juxtaposition of buildings from different historical periods, the various uses to which a building has been put—the British have a predilection for turning churches into art galleries. The ironic, the tragic, the absurd, utopias and paradises lost, all find their expression in brick and marble, concrete and steel, the presence or absence of green spaces, the breadth and layout of streets.

One of the bus routes I used to travel in London took me through Bishopgate, the area around Liverpool Street Station. In the 1980s Bishopgate was redeveloped in a typical postmodern style, an eclecticism of architectural reminiscences. The soft, rounded fronts of Dutch-style townhouses, popular in England since the seventeenth century, now were topped with large bronze cupolas normally seen on the great Italianate-style country palaces built by the English aristocracy. All of this was built in massive proportions only possible with late twentieth-century technology. Yet the references of Bishopgate are not only historical but also lateral. It is constructed with the light brown marble facings that are also so popular in Los Angeles: the Wells Fargo Center on Grand Avenue, for example. Bishopgate and the Wells Fargo Center also have the same social uses—corporate offices above smart coffee shops. Here we see a literally concrete example of the globalization of culture, predicated on a late-capitalist political economy. The political significance of these architectural embodiments of corporate confidence and pride is not lost on their British detractors. Such postmodern architecture is often referred to as Thatcherite. Margaret Thatcher herself had a keen sense of the politics of architecture and wanted to redesign No. 10 Downing Street as a microcosm of such buildings as Bishopgate's. But the architectural commission that oversees No. 10 Downing Street turned down her designs, suggesting they were more fitting in their massive proportions to the mausoleum of a great tyrant. However, one suspects that if Mrs. Thatcher had stayed in power, heads would have rolled on the architectural commission and she would have had her mausoleum.

In the vicinity of Bishopgate, there are several buildings dating from the 1960s. These buildings are functional and, their critics contend, drearily similar to each other. They were innovative in their uses of building materials, and their strict rectangularity was offset by facades that interspersed concrete with brightly painted panels. They were constructed during the postwar period of the welfare state, initiated by the Labour government elected in 1945, but also continued by the conservative governments of the 1950s and 1970s from Harold Macmillan to Edward Heath—both of whom would be to the left of the New Labour Party of Tony Blair. Unfortunately, the bold innovations in construction materials were often not successful: the brightly painted panels are faded, and many of the buildings have become structurally unsound. The closeness of Thatcherite Bishopgate to the crumbling edifices of the "New Jerusalem," as the British welfare state was also called, recapitulates recent British history. Yet during my time in London the area around Bishopgate found itself reshaped by other consequences of the British past. In 1992 the IRA's bombing campaign reached a peak, and one of the largest explosions took place in this area. The IRA's action rerouted the bus and redesigned a significant chunk of the architecture. Thatcherite Bishopgate remained unscathed—due in no small measure to the large detachment of police patrolling it.

Sometimes I took the bus to Liverpool Street or King's Cross Railway Station. There I caught a train to Cambridge to do a day's research in the university library and borrow books, or to the north of England to visit family and friends. Traveling by train is for me a very emotionally charged activity. I see train journeys as the stuff out of which so much of significance in my life was made and as a metaphor for its whole and for the lives of many of my generation.

Train journeys represent for me separation, loss, recompense, fragile continuity in the midst of change, leaving home and coming home. At eleven I began making the train journey from my small country village in the north of England to boarding school in the east of England. It was the end of my childhood and the beginning of my adolescence and an ever-widening social and geographical space for my life. It coincided with the end of the rural society and economy of my village. Increasingly the village became a dormitory for the middle classes who wanted a home in the country but worked in the nearby town of 50,000. Like many Britons of my generation, urban as well as rural, the physical and social world of our childhood had disappeared by the time we were thirty. Yet in a world of radical change, there are few things more stable than train tracks. Train lines sometimes close, but rarely does one re-track a train line. So today, in my forties, I travel the same routes on British trains that I traveled when I was five, or eleven or twenty. The same is true of Southern California. The commuter rail service is new, but the tracks date back to the nineteenth and early part of the twentieth centuries. One way of mapping social and cultural change is to compare what one sees out of a train window in the 1990s with what one would have seen in the 1960s or 1930s.

To L.A. by Rail

Having been emancipated from the automobile for a year and a half in England, you can imagine my delight on returning to Southern California in January 1993 to find that the previous fall a commuter rail service had been opened between Claremont, the town where I live, and downtown Los Angeles. Despite my love affair with trains, I had never been a rail commuter. What took me by surprise was how vastly the experience of taking public transport to Los Angeles differed from the experience of driving the freeways there.

The commuter trains are double-deckers and the upper deck offers a range of vision impossible from any freeway. When the train makes its final stop in downtown Los Angeles, I take one of the city buses, which winds through the city before reaching the University of Southern California campus. In January 1993, I felt for the first time that I was *seeing* Southern California. Apart from a limited range of vision, the freeway imposes on its travelers a geographical and social dislocation. One gets on at one entrance, and after negotiating often a maze of intersections, one gets off at another exit. You don't see the transitions in the landscape between the starting and ending point of your freeway journey. This dislocation of space has serious consequences. The commuter from a middle-class suburb to corporate downtown views his or her life as lived in oases of security amid a hostile urban world occupied by poor people, especially poor people of color. Now this phenomenon is by no means restricted to Los Angeles, but in Los Angeles it is at its most extreme. The fear and antipathy many white Angelenos feel toward poor people and people of color is exacerbated by the lack of and loss of shared physical and social space. But what is also lost is a sense of the contiguity of their space and our space, of all our spaces. This lost sense of social solidarity in Southern California is duplicated in the geographical dislocation induced by freeway travel. Thus, taking the train has the potential to expand one's social as well as physical vision. I do not want to overexaggerate the social and political benefits of train travel. If more Southern Californians had taken the train, that fact in and of itself would not have stopped the "three strikes" laws, the anti-immigrant Proposition 187, or the anti–affirmative action Proposition 23. However, the reasons people give for not taking the train are telling indicators of our social and political malaise. There is no way to travel faster between the outlying suburbs and downtown L.A. during the main rush hours than by train and connecting bus services. In addition, on the train one can read, sleep, eat, use a laptop computer, or play a Gameboy. The arguments of time, convenience, and comfort are all in favor of the train. But the objection to using the train is that one loses one's "privacy." What people most fear about taking the train is interaction with other human beings whom they might not even know. This fear is misplaced. The etiquette of privacy prevails on the train, although a certain camaraderie does develop between people who work at the same place or recognize other commonalities.

So what does one see from the train and what does it tell us about our multiple identities and locations? I begin my journey in Claremont, a college town nestled in the foothills of the San Gabriel Mountains. Although it does not have the reputation for sophistication that the west side of L.A. has, it is, as one train conductor quips, the "cappuccino capital of East Los Angeles County." It is a quiet and tasteful city—no fast-food places or overnight parking on the street, by city ordinance. It has a largely Anglo population and retains its character as a piece of New England on the edge of the Southern California desert.

The next step is Pomona—a very different city from Claremont. Minorities form the majority of its population, especially Latino but also black. Its population is largely working class and much poorer than the surrounding foothill communities. Yet in the 1950s it was a thriving blue-collar (and predominantly white) community. It was quintessential Hometown, U.S.A., and, as Kevin Starr points out, one of the early soaps of all-American family life was situated there.[1] It was a place where ordinary (white) Americans earned good wages and got their piece of the American dream. Today its city center is decayed. The large old movie theater, looking its part as a temple to popular culture and the good times of mid-century, is dilapidated and has been turned into a Hispanic evangelical church. Moviegoing is still very much part of the popular culture of Southern California; it is after all "the industry." Recently two massive cinema complexes opened in the easternmost part of the Pomona Valley, a virtual wilderness area—just about as far away as you can get from Pomona and its poor people. California always leads the way, and Kevin Starr also points out that Pomona indicates the decline of the postwar blue-collar suburb—a decline, of course, brought about by a decline in the blue-collar wage to a fraction in many cases of what it was forty years ago.

Around Pomona one passes a tract of trailer homes. Most of the homes one sees from the train are lived in by lower-income people, but not all of them. Between Pomona and the next stop, the better-off Covina, one glimpses expensive homes built in the canyons through which the rail track runs. If the track had been built in the 1990s, I'm sure it would have been diverted away from these homes. However, in the 1980s, land was scarcer and costlier than ever before, so some of the well-to-do had to put up with having their dream home next to a railway track.

After stops in Covina and Baldwin Park the train moves toward El Monte. From the train, one can read the sign "Horse Auction

Every Friday Nite." One sees stables and a white plaster statue of a horse—but only rarely live horses. These are not stud farms. They cater to the local Hispanic population. Horse riding is very important in Chicano/North Mexican culture, and the caballeros can match the Yankee cowboys in skill any day. At El Monte several professional people get off the train and step onto city-run shuttles. El Monte's social composition is similar to Pomona's, and many of the professionals who run the city prefer to live elsewhere. After El Monte a bridge carries the train high above the Los Angeles River. The Los Angeles River is a concrete-clad duct that can be completely dry for months on end. When there is water, it is usually nothing more than a thin brackish coating that rusts the wheels of the shopping carts tipped down its side. Taggers frequently embellish its concrete sides with gang insignias. However, when heavy rains come, it can turn quickly into a raging torrent. Frequently children are drowned, and many of them come from the ramshackle homes built right up to the river's brink.

Then comes the fun part of the trip. The rail track runs parallel to the freeway. The train whizzes by all those solitary drivers sitting motionless in rush-hour traffic, cherishing their privacy and their road rage. The train is even much faster than the carpool lane. One feels very smug and self-righteous gazing down on the unenlightened and unecological.

The last stop before downtown is Cal State L.A. This station was opened much later than other stations on the line because of the difficult engineering task of fitting it onto a mountainside. The other side of the track was already occupied by the freeway. However, the rumor shared among the suburban train commuters was that the proximity of Cal State L.A. to the long-established barrio of East Los Angeles had caused concern to the train authorities: riffraff and criminal elements might turn the new Metrolink train service into a horror of horrors for Southern Californians, a new version of the New York subway.

By now the train is approaching Union Station and its final destination in downtown Los Angeles. It passes through the housing projects of East Los Angeles. At one time, there was an encampment of homeless people under one of the bridges, but then one day I saw a cleanup crew from the transit authority removing all trace of their habitation. As the train nears Union Station, one is greeted by the harsh reality of the postmodern city. Two of its new landmark buildings are prisons. The county jail is visible just as one enters the station; looking toward downtown from the street in front, one can see the city jail. Every day I commute, the jails give me a visual reminder of how Mike Davis in *City of Quartz* characterizes the carceral society of Los Angeles—"this is "Fortress L.A.""[2] Having lived in California at a time when its penal system has descended into barbarism, I have come more and more to think that the old dictum of penal reform—that the state of a society can be judged from its prisons—should be central to all social analysis. Those who oppose capital punishment in particular, and the harsh and inhumane punishments of recent legislation (the "three strikes" law, the inclusion of juveniles in the adult penal system, etc.), usually appeal to the humanity, the human dignity, the value of even the worst criminal. Theologically and morally I am less concerned with the humanity of the criminal than with my own humanity. I do not want to romanticize those on death row and serving life sentences without parole as merely misguided but reformable or, in some cases, wrongly convicted.

The majority are morally vicious, but that moral viciousness is shared by those who would execute them or throw the key away. In the film *Pulp Fiction,* set in L. A., John Travolta plays a hit man who visits his heroin dealer and, while making his deal, complains that his new car has been stolen. Both the hit man and the heroin dealer agree that the law should make car theft punishable by summary execution. Perhaps Quentin Tarantino is implying a moral critique of white Angeleno and Californian society. Don't we become the moral equivalent of Tarantino's hit men and heroin dealers when we wish to impose death and suffering on others? Professionals who alter their expense accounts accept that with the "three strikes" law a person can be sent to jail for twenty five years for stealing a pizza.

Union Station is the most beautiful and stately train station I know. With its tower and lovely wooden vaulted ceiling, it is a cathedral made to the glory of rail travel. Horrifyingly, it was once nearly pulled down. The Metrolink commuter rail has been the key element in its recent revival. Now it too has that badge of urban middle-class sophistication—cappuccinos and lattes.

By Bus to Downtown

After detraining at Union Station, I make my way to the shiny new addition to Union Station, the Patsouras Transit Plaza, to catch a bus. Very few train commuters take the MTA buses, since one can also reach downtown by the new but not very extensive subway and downtown shuttle service. Hence even train commuters can avoid contact with the urban poor by using public transport systems that serve only the downtown area, where the urban poor do not live and, on the whole, do not work during the day. In the evenings when I ride the MTA bus back to Union Station after six o'clock, there are lots of largely Latino workers traveling into downtown to clean offices.

Since the USC campus lies outside the immediate downtown area, I have the options of either getting up earlier and catching the 8:00 a.m. train from Claremont, which connects with USC's own shuttle service, or taking the MTA bus with its clientele of the urban poor. Many employers run rush-hour shuttles to Union Station, which again helps suburban commuters avoid the MTA buses and the poor.

Although it's always advisable anywhere in the world to inspect a seat on public transport before sitting down on it, the MTA buses are clean. Admittedly, not all their passengers are. But only rarely have I had a smelly fellow passenger nearby—and, recalling the lecture halls of Germany on a hot summer day, I can bear it. Sometimes a fellow passenger talks in such a way that one knows he or she is missing a few marbles. Yet, quite often one's ride is made more enjoyable by the behavior of one's fellow travelers. At one bus stop, I see a mass of bright metallic balloons get on the bus; somewhere underneath them is their diminutive Hispanic vendor.

Only a few white and only a few middle-class people ride the MTA buses, and most of the middle-class riders are not white. There are elderly people speaking Chinese; and there are all sorts of Hispanic and African American bus riders, because USC lies on the border of Watts, which was a black but is now increasingly a Hispanic area. Then there are the bus drivers, drawn from every ethnic background, most of whom are saints. They treat their passengers with patience and courtesy however mentally confused they are, however broken or nonexistent their English, however shabbily dressed or malodorous they are. My stereotype of white blue-collar men as rednecks is certainly challenged by these drivers who are intelligent and caring, who have taken the trouble to learn some Spanish, and who see through the machinations of immigrant-bashing politicians.

The bus ride from Union Station to USC takes one through the most consistently postmodern architectural landscape in the world. The downtown area of L.A. is much smaller than that of Chicago or New York, and most of it was built or rebuilt during the 1980s. This means that postmodern buildings are not interspersed with others, but rather older buildings are scattered among them, enhancing rather than diluting the postmodern effect of architectural eclecticism.

This reflection on my commute was inspired by some comparisons I had made between Newark and Los Angeles. Newark's downtown is still dominated by civic buildings dating from an earlier and more prosperous time for the city. Los Angeles, on the other hand, has a postmodern downtown of corporate buildings. There are civic buildings in downtown L.A. but these are not the new postmodern ones. On First and Main streets, the bus passes the town hall, and on Grand and Sixth, one can glimpse the public library. Both of these buildings date from before the Second World War.

The architectural landscape of downtown L.A. enacts a fundamental shift in values. The space for democratic citizenship and politics and the space for public education and access to knowledge have been marginalized by the space of the market economy and global capitalization.

On the aesthetic level, I find downtown L.A.'s corporate postmodern architecture breathtakingly beautiful. On Grand Avenue I admire the Coopers Lybrand building, and if you have read Fredric Jameson's *Postmodernism, or, The Cultural Logic of Late Capitalism,* you may remember his description of L.A.'s Westin Bonaventure Hotel.[3] Jameson shares my ambivalence toward the postmodern downtown because of the political significance of this stunning aesthetic. I took a friend visiting from Zimbabwe on a tour of the downtown. Seeing the corporate names emblazoned on its magnificent buildings, he said he could not share my aesthetic appreciation of downtown L.A.: he had seen in Zimbabwe the ugliness caused by the extraction of the corporate profits that erected the postmodern architecture of Los Angeles.

A few years ago the L.A. public library was renovated and reopened. Refurbished with new technology, it is now seen as a beneficiary of the high-tech revolution carried through by the corporations that surround it. The postmodern buildings were constructed around it, but their architectural effect states the reverse. By the clever use of a cul-de-sac, and by the fluid lines and large-scale use of reflective glass, characteristic of postmodern architecture, the public library is rendered aesthetically dependent on the newer and taller construction. It has been integrated into the postmodern landscape; it has no architectural autonomy. In fact, you would believe it if someone told you that the public library, too, had been built in the 1980s as a playful, tongue-in-cheek gesture of nostalgia toward an older L.A. that had gone forever. The public library and the town hall exist—I believe through implicit intention—as residues of an older communal past, in which Angelenos held the conviction that public life should be shaped by shared political responsibility and expanding opportunities for self-improvement through learning and creativity. Such convictions and expectations may have been naïve and often disappointed, but they were both the social and physical fabric of the city Angelenos experienced. Reducing the architectural incorporations of this earlier civic culture to residues, instead of simply demolishing them, strengthens the hegemony of the corporate. Postmodern L.A. is the victory song of late capitalism. It intones, "Democracy depends on a market economy." It celebrates information as dependent on the technology the market delivers.

There is one postmodern communal space in downtown L.A.: the Museum of Contemporary Art. MOCA is built with the same light brown marble facing as the Wells Fargo Center opposite it. By the use of this internationally popular color of postmodernism, it is integrated with the corporate structures around it. I am not arguing that MOCA's architecture determines that it pursues a politics of reaction. The prevailing atmosphere there is radical chic. It is multicultural, it is innovative, and it serves a well-educated elite. Superficially, one could make the case that its cultural eclecticism is in and of itself a postmodernism of reaction. However, museums since the nineteenth century have claimed to serve everyone in their communities, from the greatest to the least. Indeed, they have made great efforts in outreach, yet their core constituency has remained middle class. Similarly, since the nineteenth century, museums have practiced cultural eclecticism; in fact, museums often acted as repositories for the booty from colonial conquest. The distinctively postmodern location of MOCA is in the global commodification of culture. There is a market for everything—even multiculturalism, even politically radical art. MOCA also attests to the hegemony of a global capitalist economy.

Having traveled down Grand Avenue past MOCA and the Wells Fargo Center and the public library on a cross street, the bus turns onto Eleventh Street. To the north is the postmodern downtown separated by parking lots from the south side of Eleventh Street and its sweatshops. One could pass these sweatshops a hundred times and not know that they were there. Only on the hottest of summer days, when the temperature hits 100 degrees and the workers inside must be on the verge of collapse, are the doors of these establishments opened. From the bus, one catches a quick glimpse of their interiors. Dingily lit and without windows, these concrete buildings house Asian and Latino women cramped around work tables and sewing machines.

However, downtown L.A. would like to displace the poor farther away from its center. Plans have been devised by the city government, corporations, and USC that foresee corporate L.A. expanding southward and USC expanding northward. Already, at Olympic and Figueroa, the new convention center has been constructed, which covers several tens of acres. From the bus, it is visible to the right, but to the left, the squat buildings of warehouses and factories remain.

Soon after, the bus reaches the USC campus. Originally built in the nineteenth century, it was part of an upscale and much smaller

L.A., populated with upper-class transplants from the East Coast and Midwest. Today it is an oasis of privilege in a sea of Hispanics and African Americans struggling for economic survival, a struggle made increasingly difficult by the policies of USC. USC is the largest employer in the city. It draws its janitors, food service workers, and other support staff from the poor minority communities that surround it. In recent years, it has increasingly removed such workers from its payroll, replacing their labor through subcontractors. The same people continue to work at USC but are no longer its employees. The consequences are that these people have lost their benefits and that new staff are hired by the subcontractors at substantially lower wages than the university itself paid. The university has also colluded with one of its subcontractors to fight the attempts of janitors to unionize themselves. You may think that after the L.A. unrest of 1992 and considering USC's geographical location, self-interest would dictate at least a benevolent paternalism. There is plenty of paternalism but little benevolence. USC has instead decided to fortify its campus with tall iron railings.

Evening Rush Hour

If I leave by 5:50 in the afternoon, I can take a USC shuttle back to Union Station. The traffic flow of L.A. means that during evening rush hour, it is quicker for the shuttle to take the surface streets rather than the freeway. Its route skirts the eastern edge of the downtown area. This is a predominantly Hispanic area, although there is also some Asian presence, especially in the garment district. This is also what many Anglos fear. Their city—forget L.A.'s Mexican origins—is being turned into Latin America. It is difficult to avoid learning Spanish here: we pass a music store called "el ritmo Latino" and numerous *agencias de viajes* (travel agencies). A sign picturing a flock of sheep proclaims how much money can be won this week in the lottery—*catorce million dolares es mucho lana.*

So far I've not mentioned any churches on my route. From the train on a smogless day, one can see the spire of my own church in Claremont silhouetted against the mountains. On the evening shuttle, we are driven up Main Street. Its central section is a red-light district with XXX-rated movie theaters and cheap hotels. The impression of squalor is overwhelming there. We are close to the corporate downtown, and one suspects that during the lunch hour, corporate executives and professionals come over here for a quick trick. However, by early evening, they've gone home or to more upscale establishments of sexual entertainment. At this hour, even the johns seem to be working-class minority men. At the top end of the red-light district is St. Vibiana's Roman Catholic Cathedral. Its building is not in much better repair than the dilapidated brothels and sex movie theaters down the street. In fact, St. Vibiana's is about to be demolished and a new cathedral built on a more morally salubrious site next to the L.A. Music Center. This move has been highly controversial. Cardinal Mahoney has been accused of hypocrisy, professing solidarity with the poor and at the same time deserting them. The nineteenth-century cathedral, despite its antiquity—by L.A. standards—has no architectural merit and is structurally unsafe. However, the decision was made not to rebuild a cathedral in the existing location, and the character of the surrounding area influenced that decision. Already the diocesan offices have moved to another location because the safety of its workers— especially women—could not be ensured. One can joke about nuns being propositioned as prostitutes, but it was impossible to work or hold programs there in the evening after dark. Nonetheless, the disappearance of St. Vibiana's does mean that the church is going to be less visible in an area where one can read despair, emptiness, impoverishment, and deprivation on the faces of most people on its streets.

From St. Vibiana's to Union Station is a small distance, and so this is my final stop on a reflective journey to work and back in Los Angeles. What have I learned in L.A. and London about the relationship of theology to the urban architectural landscape?

I think I have learned something about incarnation, the ability of our humanity to be God-bearing and to signify the divine. Contemporary critiques and revisions of the doctrine of incarnation have stressed two things. First, they have objected to the anthropocentrism of the traditional doctrine of the incarnation, arguing that it has devalued nonhuman creation by denying to it the presence of the divine.[4] Second, they have found earlier formulations of the doctrine inadequate because they excluded our bodies from full divinity.[5] Christ may have assumed a human body, but this was to gain and heal our mental and spiritual qualities. After the cross, Christ discards or substitutes an ordinary human body for one made up of imperishable and immortal stuff. The current theological emphasis on our ordinary embodied selves' ability to signify the divine counteracts this tradition.

However salutary a corrective this reworking of the doctrine of incarnation has been in these two areas, it leaves certain issues unaddressed. What is the physical space of our humanity? I would claim not just flesh and blood, muscle and membrane, but also concrete and brick, steel and glass. Our minds do not directly interact with each other outside of our bodies. Nor do our bodies interact directly with each other outside of physical space. Our selves, our identities and subjectivities, are dispersed through a physical space much greater than our bodies. Our bodies are not just part of a broader natural environment, they are also a cultural artifact constantly circulating within physical human culture. The city is not a mere container for our selves; it is ourself. Its urban architectural landscape is what we look like.

We often prefer to see ourselves in physical continuity with the natural environment, at one with wind and wave, tree and flower. This sensibility has been fostered by a growing ecological consciousness among theologians. The city was—from the book of Revelation and Augustine to Harvey Cox's *Secular City*—the site of human encounter with God. The city was a metaphor for spiritual destiny and the ultimate fulfillment or failure of human life. Recently, in part due to the ecological emphasis, the city has fallen out of the theological imagination or been reduced to one side of the Augustinian dualism, the *civitas terrena*. Earthly city or, more likely, city of quartz, it has become a metonym for the postmodern condition, symbol and part of the end of history and end of the human.

In this postmodern condition, the Christian churches often prefer to revert to their origins and play an escape from the world, not from our bodies but from their urban reality. In antiquity Christianity began and was able to thrive as a religion situated in the household, in domestic space. Eventually it was even able to attract large numbers of freeborn male citizens because of the decline of the ancient polis in the Roman Empire and the sense of political disenfranchisement that this engendered. Today, amid a loss of democratic culture and the atrophy of democratic citizenship, a similar sense of political disenfranchisement prevails. A major response of the churches, mainline as well as evangelical, is to locate themselves in a public domestic space. The church is a macrocosm of the family. The oxymoronic designation of the church as public domestic space and extension of the family certainly has its origins in modernity. What has changed is that church no longer mediates between the domestic and civic. Instead, it has become a site for the reprivatization of the civic. One example of this is government's shifting of social welfare back to the churches.

The processes that marginalize democratic citizenship are synergistic with those of a global commodification of culture. For everything there is a market. One successful commodity in postmodern society is spirituality. Does theology have a role in resisting the commodification of the spirit?

I am not going to conclude by taking the other side of the Augustinian dualism. London and Los Angeles are not cities of God. But those of us who are citizens of that other city need to recognize the God-bearing capacity of our earthly cities. Just as the present hegemony of a global capitalist economy is not the end of history, the corporate postmodern culture is not our ultimate cultural destiny. Beyond modernity there are other ways of resignifying our humanity and rebuilding our cities. These are also theological tasks.

Postscript

This essay was written in the late 1990s, and the urban landscape and transport systems of Los Angeles have seen many changes since then. I decided not to update the main body of the essay but to leave it as a snapshot of its specific historical period. In Los Angeles three major public buildings have been completed—the Staples stadium (home of the Lakers basketball team), the Disney Concert

Hall, and the new Roman Catholic cathedral. The names of the first two underscore how corporations dominate cultural life and how their patronage shapes the civic landscape as extensively as that of kings, aristocrats, popes, and bishops have done in European cities of the past. In this context Cardinal Mahoney's cathedral seems like a throwback to an earlier age. However, despite all the jokes about Taj Mahoney, entry to the cathedral is free, and its artwork and architecture celebrate the ethnic diversity of Los Angeles. Most of the side chapels are used to provide temporary space for the religious celebrations of the various ethnic communities. Across the Atlantic the Labour Party government in Britain also realized the importance of open access to public cultural sites and abolished admission charges for museums and art galleries. Before Tony Blair gave in to militarist delusions, his government embarked on perhaps the greatest program of public works in British history. London and the major cities have received spectacular new buildings such as the Great Court of the British Museum and the Sage Gateshead, but more significantly small industrial towns with working class populations have also been renewed with fine renovations and new construction of public buildings. It can be rightly argued that Los Angeles' cathedral and the British program of public works do not make a dent on global capitalism. Nonetheless, the public enthusiasm for these buildings that are accessible to all shows that there is still a widespread hunger for shared communal space. How we use and perceive space also depends on how we travel from one place to another. Two labor disputes in Los Angeles, which stopped the buses and the still meager subway system for several weeks, showed how much the poor rely on public transport. Without the buses to get them to work, many lost their jobs or had to pay high fares to taxis and private shuttles that they could not really afford. Poor high school students could often not get to their schools. After 9/11 there is an increased awareness of the vulnerability of American cities but not of the inequities in infrastructure that mark them. During the Los Angeles transport strike in 2003 free shuttles were provided for the middle-class suburban train commuters to get them to their downtown offices; no provision was made for low-income bus riders.

It is easier said than done to think further theologically about the God-bearing capacity of our cities. If we think of cities incarnating God in our humanity, then crucifixion and resurrection are manifest in their inextricably connected physical and social infrastructure. This shares the frailty of our human flesh, which is vulnerable to attack and to neglect and decay. Yet our cities also can participate in the resurrection of the body. They can be physically transformed and renewed so that the peace and justice of the city of God resides within them. In the new cathedral in Los Angeles the altar tapestries map the streets of contemporary Los Angeles onto the oval plan associated with the New Jerusalem. They are inscribed with words from Revelation 21:3: "See, God's dwelling is among mortals. God will dwell with them. They will be God's people and God will be with them." These tapestries continue a long tradition of incorporating theological ideas into the physical fabric of sacred buildings. More difficult is the reverse movement from physical space, whether sacred or secular, to theological expression. Theological language does not have to be verbal, and theologians do not need to leave the visual expression of theological ideas entirely to artists. Multimedia and digital cinematography can be among our tools as theologians, allowing us to combine written and spoken texts with images and sound that can better represent the relationship of theological reflection to our physical identity with the city. Furthermore, these new media encourage us to think visually so that even our conventionally produced theological texts can be aware of space and light, line and color, the complex interaction of physical space with the individual and collective imagination.

The construction of a new theological vocabulary is essentially a political task. If we make a visual argument about how space is used and traversed in our cities, then we can challenge the contemporary self-description of Christian churches as family and as public domestic space. The *familia* or household of the ancient world and early Christianity was not a domestic realm divorced from the political. The early Christian "household of God" also described itself in the language of a political assembly, the *ecclesia*. The public domesticity of the churches can be replaced by an understanding of them as local spaces of the political within their cities, the meaning of *oikos* (household) in ancient political theory. Not only theological ideas but also political values can and are incorporated in church architecture. Democratic citizenship can be physically built into our ecclesial spaces, which can be models for the broader *ecclesia* of the civic community. Admittedly, local Christian communities are often far from promoting such an ideal. But a necessary component of theology is utopia, the ability to think critically about the social and physical places that emplot our lives by measuring them against the ideal place that actually exists nowhere. Utopia can also be an alternative name for the invisible church. The invisible church is thus to be conceived, not as the number of authentic Christians but as the extension of God's incarnation in our humanity. From this location we can be engaged in the attempt to make visible in physical and imagined space through concrete and glass as well as text and digital image that other city, the New Jerusalem, the city of God among the corporate pride and fragile infrastructure of the earthly city of the angels and all the other postmodern urban landscapes.

2
A Theologian in the Factory
Toward a Theology of Social Transformation
in the United States
M. Shawn Copeland

This reflection emerges from my firm conviction that African American theologians, indeed, theologians from oppressed and marginalized communities for whom this land is home, ought to assume responsibility for a theology of social transformation in the United States.[1] The articulation of such a theology finds its starting point in the real sufferings and aspirations, the cultural and social experiences—political, economic, technological—and the living faith of those marginated women and men deemed expendable in others' mindless pursuit of power, profit, and pleasure. That articulation provides a critical mediation of the Christian gospel: it contests not only egregious, vicious, sinful instances of racism, sexism, and class exploitation in a capitalist system of production, but addresses the psychological and affective agonies that suffuse modern human living as well. That articulation is tutored by critical historical accounts of the arrivals, encounters, and migrations of the rich cultures and peoples who simultaneously clash and coalesce, delight and perplex, offend and uplift one another in the constitution and realization of the compound complex of operations and coopera- tions, relations and interrelations, values and practices that is the United States of America.[2] A theology of social transformation aims to apprehend and understand the cultural and social matrices com- prehensively.[3] That articulation supplies an analysis of the religious, intellectual, and moral horizons within which emerge the various meanings and values by which women and men constitute (or fail to constitute) themselves as authentic human persons and realize (or fail to realize) their society as a place that fosters the flourishing of life. While no theological formulation is ever a substitute for empirical social science, a theology of social transformation advo- cates and forwards the concrete possibility of intelligent and rea- sonable solutions to human problems, while unfolding the higher viewpoint of the divine solution to suffering and evil. That articula- tion promotes and stipulates social praxis, but it neither recklessly nor romantically embraces activism. Moreover, such a theology advocates not for some extrinsic or artificial correlation between human living and the experience of faith, but a praxis that emerges from, and is consonant with, a community of faith. That theologi- cal articulation stands as an integration of the natural and super- natural ends of human living; it brings out and confesses the continuity of those ends; it adverts explicitly to the concrete prac- tices, meanings, and manifestations that disclose the Spirit's gift of grace. It goes without saying that such a theology of social transfor- mation approximates a politically responsible methodical theology.

How might such a theology of social transformation be con- structed? The concrete starting point for this reflection is the tragedy that is the city of Detroit.[4] More specifically, let us focus on the automobile factory as a key institution in the breakdown of the recurrent schemes that constitute the social order. This chapter's four parts will examine several dimensions of the problem. First, to come to terms with the "crisis of the human good" of which Detroit is but one instance, the city must be seen in the context of the mas- sive breakdown in the social order. Second, the city's history, growth, and expansion may be seen in terms of Bernard Lonergan's category of emergent probability in human affairs. The social and cultural themes presented here are best read as suggestive or illustrative, rather than exhaustive, although my aim is comprehensive. What I hope is that we will be encouraged to ask and answer questions about the progress (or decline) of the human good in relation to the cities we love.

Third, we will examine the automobile factory. Why the automobile factory?[5] In the city of Detroit, the automobile factory is the key locus of the intersection of the progress (or decline) of the "social good of order" in all its technological, economic, political, cultural complexity.[6] Focus on the factory provides an opportunity to grasp the dynamic process and effect of progress (or decline) of practical intelligence in the technological order. Moreover, focus on the factory affords a unique perspective on the ways in which true values are incarnated or not, on the ways in which bias is contested or not, on the ways in which the human good—even on the scale of a city—is fostered or retarded. A politically responsible methodical theology of social transformation through serious study of the factory and its components can help the church to encourage, perhaps even to facilitate, the practical and intelligent collaboration of economists, labor leaders, factory workers, and managers in grasping, understanding, critically deciding upon, and creating conditions for growth and progress. Moreover, such a theology can go a long way in identifying and working to exclude the distorting effects of bias in this process. Here we will examine the shifts in meaning of personal relations, of valuing human persons in the factory, and of the role of unions.

Finally, we will briefly meditate on the divine or transcendent solution to the problem of evil. This is not an effort to obviate social praxis, but to apprehend it as also flawed and capable of misinterpretation; yet we can never abandon our human freedom nor relinquish our responsibility for the human situation.

One Land, Two Americas

We women and men of the North[7] live without thinking. The dimensions and depth of our global crisis involve contradictions that result from bias, from alienations of intelligence. In our short-sighted and frenetic drive to technological innovation and improvement, mere bloat in the economic order passes for growth. The political order, equally shortsighted, is eager for a ready-made solution and requires that novelty be the product of progress. These conditions are rooted in our failure at the reflexive level of culture to adhere to the norms of developed, disinterested intelligence; to reflect sufficiently on the implications, meanings, and values that are generated, conditioned, and realized in every exercise of concrete practical intelligence; and to identify and promote those meanings and values that foster human flourishing. Tissa Balasuriya is correct: when we fail to live and when we fail to act without thinking, we reveal ourselves as "civilized barbarians."[8] The resultant accumulation of oversights, of alienations of intelligence, of failures to reflect critically, and of refusals to transcend bias constitute the longer cycle of decline. Two of the symptoms of that cycle are over- and under-development.

Overdevelopment is engrossed by and requires underdevelopment.[9] The conditions of poverty, dependence, and deprivation that consign more and more of the inhabitants of our planet to a living death, are not just somewhere else—they are readily observable in any city in the United States. Fifteen years ago, social theorists alerted us to the "Latin Americanization" of the United States, the obsolescence of unskilled and skilled labor, and the corporation's increasing loyalty to its profit margin rather than to the common human good of the nation, state, or city in which it operates.[10] The dynamics of underdevelopment within our overdeveloped society have created internal colonies in which vital needs go unsatisfied—food, shelter, clothing, functional literacy, health care, cultural development, human dignity and self-respect. It is not difficult to map these racial, cultural, political, and economic colonies—Dorchester and Roxbury, Massachusetts; the South Bronx and Harlem, New York; South Side Chicago and Cairo, Illinois; Hartford and Bridgeport and New Haven, Connecticut; East St. Louis, Missouri; the Hill District in Pittsburgh, Pennsylvania; and Detroit, Michigan.

There are then at least two Americas—one *overdeveloped*: privileged, educated, predominantly white, but including (partially) members of other races, and possessing the economic, political, and ideological means to sustain and justify a way of life that restricts the common good to merely "an identity of interest";[11] the other *underdeveloped*: marginalized, segregated, poorly educated if at all, overwhelmingly black, brown, and red, but including members of other races, and deprived of the economic and political means to create and sustain a way of life that participates in the realization of the common human good. Consider that the poorest fifth of households in the United States collect only 4 percent of the national income, while the richest fifth receive nearly half.[12] Consider the disastrous and conflicting results of "populist distrust of remote political institutions coupled with the tax revolt which undercuts basic community services and opposes social innovation."[13] Consider these statistics:

> The poverty rate of female-headed families was 36.3 percent in 1982, while the rate for married-couple families was only 7.6 percent. For black and Spanish-origin female-headed families in 1982, poverty rates were 56.2 percent and 55.4 percent respectively.
>
> Forty-six percent of all poor families and 71 percent of all poor black families were female headed in 1982. These proportions were higher for metropolitan areas, particularly for central cities, where 60 percent of all poor families and 78 percent of all poor black families were headed by women. . . . The proportion of poor white families headed by women also increased from less than 20 percent in 1959 to a high of almost 40 percent in 1977, and then dropping to 35 percent in 1983.
>
> Between 1947 and 1972, the central cities of the thirty-three most populous metropolitan areas (according to 1970 figures) lost 800,000 manufacturing jobs, while manufacturing employment in their suburbs grew by 2.5 million. The same cities lost 867,000 jobs in retail and wholesale trade at the same time their suburbs gained millions of such positions. While the black populations of these central cities were growing substantially, white and middle-class residents migrated to the suburbs. Between 1950 and 1980, populations in these central cities lost more than 9 million whites and added more than 5 million blacks, many of them from the rural South.[14]

Consider that the poor in the United States are disproportionately exposed to pollution and hazardous materials.

> Neighborhood-by-neighborhood comparisons of income level, race, and toxic waste site location reveal a disturbing but not so surprising pattern. The poorer the neighborhood, and the darker the skin of its residents, the more likely it is to be near a toxic waste dump. Three-fourths of hazardous waste landfills in the American Southeast are in low-income, black neighborhoods, and more than half of all black and Hispanic Americans live in communities with at least one toxic waste site.[15]

The longer cycle of our decline is manifest in anarchistic materialism; in the obsolescence of skilled industrial and factory workers; in increased and unreflective reliance on automation; in the rising disposability not only of objects or products, but of roles, tasks, skills—hence, in the disposability of the men and women who perform those roles, tasks, and skills. This decline is disclosed in the rise of white supremacy and the mounting boldness of groups that militaristically promote it; in the vulgar as well as subtle displays of sexism; in the physical and psychological assaults on gay men and lesbians. This decline is uncovered in the very invisibility of the indigenous peoples of North America. It is revealed in the sharpened public anxiety about family life; in egregious genetic experimentation; in artificial intimacy, in the frenetic, orgiastic, and suicidal use of sex, alcohol, and drugs. This decline is exposed in the ingenious exploitation of the various media of communication to manipulate, to shape, and to control human development without full human consent; in the visceral, gratuitous, and vicarious indulgence in violence in movies, television programs, and sports; in the substitution of "Newspeak" for dialogue and conversation; in the deformation of the imagination; in the cultivation of the pornographic mind. The condition of our decline is laid bare most poignantly in the unmistakable, if unvoiced, yearning for some form of social or secular redemption.

One City, Three or Four Worlds

In writing about Detroit, Edmund Wilson identified the city as a microcosm of "the whole structure of an industrial society."[16] In 1974 Robert Conot, in *The American Odyssey*, commented on the city's national as well as international ties:

As the world center of the automobile industry, it has exerted tremendous social and economic influence. It has been the head-quarters of two of the world's largest corporations, and it is America's most unionized city. Detroit is the heart of American industry, and by the beat of that heart much of America's economic health is measured.[17]

B. J. Widick echoed a similar refrain: "As Detroit goes, so goes the country."[18] Quite likely, Wilson, Conot, and Widick would agree with Lynda Ewen's assessment that Detroit is a city in crisis.[19] And if Detroit remains the bellwether of the economic and political health of the United States, then, clearly this country is quite ill. For even the most cursory contact with the city of Detroit painfully discloses the breakdown not only in the technological, economic and political orders, but in the development of the human mind, the human heart, and the human spirit. In this factory town, we are patently confronted by the longer cycle of decline.

Emergent Probability in Human Affairs:
The City and the Automobile

The principal colonial cities of North America were designed as part of a "feeder system that provided raw materials for the home-land and a limited market for manufactured goods."[20] Founded in 1701 by Antoine de la Mothe Cadillac, Fort Pontchartrain du Detroit, the city of Detroit was an extension of Montreal and the French maritime settlements of the North Atlantic coast. Its function was military, and its military objective was economic in order to protect the French fur trade from incursions by the English and the Iroquois whom they had made their allies.

The French brought to Detroit the *seigneurial* system of the *ancien régime*, refashioning it but little to the customs and environ-mental factors of North America. As commandant and *seigneur*, Cadillac was literally a feudal lord. As *seigneur*, he named vassals and granted them land, but he reserved for himself the rights to the minerals, timber, firewood, and stone on a vassal's fief or land. What is astonishing is that this social system was imposed fifty years after Massachusetts settlers "had abandoned communal land tenure and moved toward a modernized form of holding landed wealth: freehold tenure."[21] Cadillac not only held monopolies on the gristmill and on the sale of gunpowder, wine, and brandy, he also licensed and regulated all commerce and trade. Cadillac and his associates dominated the lucrative and essential fur trade, since nearly all beaver pelts were shipped under the seal of the *seigneur*. This system hobbled agricultural self-sufficiency, prohibited the residents of Detroit from engaging in free trade with Montreal, and hampered cultural and political adaptation.[22]

The population, dominated by the French, grew slowly for the first fifty years. In 1760 some 500 to 600 people lived in Detroit, and in 1810 only 770. But the steady immigration of the Irish, Germans, New Yorkers, and New Englanders, "strict sober-sides from the land of Jonathan Edwards,"[23] aided by the completion of the Erie Canal in 1825, made the population heterogeneous and pushed it to approximately 9,000 by 1838.[24]

The canal efficiently and economically moved the Northwest's products through the Great Lakes to the East; when the Canadian Welland Canal opened, the Great Lakes were connected to the St. Lawrence. Vessels took flour, tobacco, cider, and salted fish to the East and returned with oysters and manufactured goods. Detroit began to prosper and city leaders aimed to make it a key Midwestern commercial center. The final two decades of the nineteenth century were decisive years for Detroit: the population reached 286,000 and would rise to nearly half a million by 1910; the city doubled its land area; its industrial base was diversified. And one July afternoon in 1899, William Murphy and Henry Ford drove the triangular route of some sixty miles from Detroit to Farmington to Pontiac and back in a car that Ford had built.[25]

Robert Conot emphasizes that it is important to look further than Henry Ford to understand why Detroit became the chief site of automobile manufacturing in the United States. By the mid-nineteenth century, the city had attained a high level of mercantile development. It was the center of the Erie lakeshore region's petroleum industry (Pennsylvania, Ohio, and Indiana), and the city's shipbuilding experience gave it a considerable edge in developing internal combustion technology. And just as railroad expansion had slowed, the automobile industry was growing. Men (and women) were looking for work, and the seventy auto manufacturers recruited widely, bringing them from Europe, Canada, and all over the United States to Detroit.

> For better than a half century the city had been a major production center. The technology for manufacturing frames, bodies, wheels, axles, and bearings was developed. From the vast deposits of chemicals and salt came the ingredients that were turned into paint and glass. The cheapness and availability of lumber had made southeastern Michigan into the hub of the American carriage-building industry; and in the first two decades of automobile construction wood was used for bodies and wheels. The carriage industry had developed a skilled force of leather workers, upholsterers, and carpenters, all of whom were able to transfer their skills to the making of automobiles.[26]

This process as Conot recounts it is a good example of Lonergan's notion of emergent recurrent schemes in nature and in human affairs. Practical intelligence, human ingenuity, inventive expertise, and financial capital coalesced. Ransom Olds, Charles B. King, Oliver Barthel, Henry Ford, Henry Leland, and John and Horace Dodge, among others, provided the city with technological expertise in designing and building the internal combustion engine; moreover their interaction—at once collaborative, competitive, and conflictive—also refined that technology and sparked ongoing experimentation. The idea must be translated from the inventor's intelligently disciplined imagination to the blueprint. Building an automobile required availability and convenient access to raw materials; once at hand, the raw materials needed processing; once processed, the materials must be molded to the design. Men and women—skilled workers of every kind—were needed in Detroit: "tailors, painters, carpenters, machinists, furniture makers, bicycle mechanics, metalworkers, glaziers."[27] Unskilled workers came as well. Men and women left the copper mines and forests of upper Michigan, the coal mines of West Virginia, the hills of Appalachia, the mean sharecropping system of Georgia, the societies grown static in Italy and Hungary and Ireland.

By 1919 the basic elements of twentieth-century Detroit were fixed. The automobile industry brought sharply fluctuating business cycles. One writer put it descriptively, but ever so tellingly: "When the national economy was beset by a cold, Detroit normally caught pneumonia."[28] Not surprisingly, the factories determined the economic and class structure of Detroit, stamping it with a working-class or blue-collar character.[29] Even more important, automobile manufacturing left an emphatic imprint on the political and cultural temperament of Detroit. The industry "influenced the city's language and metaphors, the subjects treated in its newspapers and magazines, and its law enforcement practices."[30] Detroit advertised itself as "The Motor City." And the industry even penetrated the churches, most directly in Henry Ford's plan "to recruit carefully selected Negro workmen" through the recommendations of black clergy.[31]

The 1930s saw the rise of a new union, the United Automobile Workers (UAW). In 1937 the union made shrewd use of the sitdown strike against General Motors to curb the overweening power the manufacturers had wielded over the workers. This action proved to be the turning point for organizing mass-production workers into unions.[32] But forty years later, the union would be more a tool of the company than a protection for the worker. Walter Reuther, a founder and president of the UAW, once declared, "We make collective bargaining agreements, not revolutions."[33] And by the late 1960s, the UAW had grown distant from the mass of workers, especially blacks and women. While at least 30 percent of the union membership was black and 14 percent women, its twenty-six-member executive board numbered only two black males and one white female.[34]

In Detroit, research meant only one thing—the new automobile design for the production year. In the 1950s, industry leaders consciously hampered scientific investigation into the new electronic and computer-related technologies that would have permitted the city to diversify and achieve a more balanced economic base. By refusing to encourage or reward theoretical or scientific research, by preferring to concentrate human and technical resources exclusively on the development of the automobile, they also undercut human (intellectual) development and squandered human potential. The automobile manufacturers opted for short-term common-sense solutions, failing to calculate the long-term consequences.

In the summer of 1967, rebellions flared in black communities in cities throughout the United States including Tampa, Cincinnati, Atlanta, Newark, and Detroit.[35] The violence in Detroit was the worst in the nation: 41 people, most of them black, were shot by police and National Guardsmen; 347 people were injured; 3,800 people were arrested; whole neighborhoods were burned, leaving some 5,000 children, women, and men homeless; 1,300 buildings were torched and 2,700 business ransacked.[36] The impact was dramatic. Within weeks, sometimes days, whites sold their homes and moved to outlying areas; businesses closed all along the main avenues of the city; suburban real estate developers reaped profits. Yet while it seemed sudden, the impact only dramatized the city's old inequities. There were, and had been since the early part of the century, several worlds that constituted the city of Detroit: one corporate and increasingly international; another comfortable, prosperous, catered to by the sophisticated downtown shopping district (now an abandoned shell); a third blue-collar, white poly-ethnic, Arab, and black, buffeted by the economic turbulence of the automobile industry; and a fourth poor, overwhelmingly black, and seething with discontent.

The Factory

The factory is an institution of technology within a concrete social order. It is a recurrent scheme conditioned by organic, psychic, and intellectual development; by the operation of practical skills; by the cooperations that bring forth various divisions of labor, roles, and tasks. The factory may or may not contribute to the rise of the "social good of order." When the factory malfunctions, when its workers (individual men and women) fail to assume or are prevented from assuming responsibility for their various roles, when they fail to cooperate or are prevented from cooperating in the performance of their various tasks, a component of the social good of order breaks down. At the same time, the social good of order ought not to be subordinated to, identified or confused with the various institutions (such as factories, schools, banks, and political parties or systems) that contribute to its emergence and maintenance. Indeed, the social good of order goes beyond such institutions. It is the result of the skills, the expertise, the resourcefulness, the commitment, the pride, the cooperation, and the mutual human regard of a whole people who intelligently, imaginatively, and creatively adapt and change to varying circumstances and events in the constitution of the human good. And the human good emerges in the struggling effort of a whole people to master the drift toward disorder and to realize true instances of vital, social, cultural, personal, and religious value.[37]

Personal Relations

The most effective way to understand and to evaluate the factory is to attend not to the recurrent schemes by which it manufactures a flow of particular goods, but rather to attend to, understand, and evaluate the state of its personal relations.[38] In the first decade of the twentieth century, Frederick Winslow Taylor, a prototype of the modern efficiency expert, prepared a set of recommendations for automobile manufacturers seeking to increase factory productivity. "Taylorizing" a plant required that managers plan every worker's task: the manner in which it was to be performed and the amount of time needed. The old-style foreman, who hired and knew the men who worked under him and who often held their respect, was replaced by several "efficiency experts—an inspector, a gang boss, a speed boss, a repair boss, a time clerk, a route clerk, and a disciplinarian."[39] With Taylorization factories sucked in "the young, the strong, the healthy—the most productive third of the work force" and spewed out the aging, the weakened, the worn, the slow, and the disabled. When asked what would happen to these discarded workers, Taylor replied, "They would find work elsewhere—sooner or later."[40]

In regard to the importance of personal relations to the realization of the human good, I make three observations. First, the old guild relationship between an apprentice and a master already had been overturned by the "putting-out system" that changed the guild master to an independent contractor. But under industrialization the guild master became a foreman: an agent not of aesthetics and ethics, but of efficiency chiefly. Under the guild system, the apprentice was valued for his practical intelligence, for the development of his skill, for his painstaking mastery of craft. The new Taylorized factory system valued him only for his brute strength; any skill that was needed could be acquired in a matter of weeks. Should business slow, he could be dismissed and then easily rehired or replaced. The factory boss's relation to him came not from an inheritance of life in a shared community with shared values, but from the expedient efficiency of production.

Second, for generations the guild system had sought to foster respect and regard among masters and apprentices. Some masters abused their apprentices and took advantage of their service, yet the ideal neither sanctioned nor acquiesced to such behavior. From the outset the new factory system generated antagonistic relations between the workers and the various bosses. And the bosses exploited the mutual suspicion and fear that hampered relations between diverse ethnic groups.

Henry Ford further manipulated this climate of suspicion and fear to socially engineer "the most disciplined work force since the beginning of the Industrial Revolution."[41] Within his company Ford organized a "Sociology Department" to monitor and mold the conduct of the workers and control their pay. Investigators from the Sociology Department visited workers' homes checking whether beds were made up, and sometimes inspecting savings account passbooks or demanding an itemization of household debts.[42]

> Fellow workers, neighbors, wives, children, and even the doctors of workers were interviewed. Each scrap of information, each piece of gossip was entered on a card in the man's name, and filed. The Sociology Department bred suspicion, mistrust, and silence. Through the department, men could exploit their grudges; wives could coerce their husbands; neighbors, landlords, and creditors could threaten.[43]

A worker who violated the established codes by smoking cigarettes, consuming excessive alcohol, suffering marital discord, or gambling found his pay reduced. If after six months the worker had still not reformed, he was discharged. Since employment at Ford Motor Company was highly sought after, workers submitted to these investigations. But it robbed them and their families of pride and the freedom to struggle with and create their own lives.

Ford went further. On January 5, 1914, Henry Ford and James Couzens announced "the eight-hour, $5, profit sharing day."[44] Its economic practicality was cloaked under altruism: the Sociology Department was to certify just which *family men* were deemed eligible and worthy of the five-dollar day. Women workers averaged $2.07 a day; male probationers who had not yet demonstrated their moral fitness earned $2.72 a day. Perceptively, Conot writes:

> While businessmen exaggeratedly denounced Ford, social workers went to the other extreme and hailed him as a paragon, the new industrialist with a social conscience. No one understood what Ford meant when he called the $5 day a "piece of efficiency engineering, too." No one paid notice to the firing of nine hundred Orthodox Greeks and Russians who had thrown the plant into an uproar by celebrating Christmas in January. No one grasped the implication of Ford's statement that his workers "must observe American customs and holidays." No one looked beyond Ford's altruistic proclamation of "social justice," or examined how the rules laid down to make men eligible for that social justice would benefit the company.[45]

No one grasped that Ford had introduced the five-dollar–a-day wage to stave off the organizing efforts of the Industrial Workers of the World (IWW), which had been leading strikes against dangerous mining conditions in upper Michigan.[46]

Third, a correlate of personal relations is personal status. The new factory system, particularly under Taylorization, conceptualized the human person as an object, a means of labor power. The workers were treated as things because one can more easily coordinate things than persons. Moreover, each worker was interchangeable with every other (young, strong, and healthy) worker: the new factory system dealt with the requirements of skilled or semiskilled roles—die cutter, machinist—and not with persons. The worker entered the factory as another line item in the cost of pro-duction. Hence the distinction between the role and the person was introduced, and the worker was beset with feelings of worthless-ness, loss of self-esteem, and injured dignity.[47]

Faced with increasing objectification and virtually assured of being replaced by a machine, faced with the squalor of pinched liv-ing in unsanitary boardinghouses or tenements, the inquisitorial eye of the social worker, and the absence of recreative outlets, many workers and their families collapsed under the alienation and isola-tion, the confusion and bewilderment. Some who had left farms and rural communities never adjusted to the anonymity and imper-sonality of the growing urban environment and succumbed to mental and physical diseases: schizophrenia, pneumonia, tubercu-losis, malnutrition, alcoholism. Others, equally adrift, found them-selves in a web of debt or prostitution or crime.

Frederick Winslow Taylor changed the nature of labor, Henry Ford changed its meaning and value, but modern technology has changed its scope. Let me extend the discussion of the worker's loss of personal status by noting two very modern technological inno-vations in production that have become quite commonplace.

> The first is the technology for conquering distance—container-ized shipping, jet air-cargo carriers, telecommunications systems, etc. The second is the technology for fragmenting the productive process into a variety of component operations that can be per-formed across the planet at different production sites and then reintegrated into a global product. . . . Quantities of leather cov-ers, yarn, thread, and cement made in the U.S. are shipped to Haiti, where local women, at wage rates as low as any in the hemisphere, assemble them into baseballs.[48]

This widespread geographic diffusion of the production process exploits "an inexhaustible supply of cheap labor."[49] Multinational corporations have transmuted these workers into increasingly cru-cial forms of capital. Not only does such piecework alienate the worker from the product (from the whole or a sense of the whole), it alienates the worker from a sense of the dignity and meaning of work, a sense of one's own work as dignified and meaningful.

Valuing Human Persons in the Factory

The factory values efficiency, productivity, and profitability. Over the long term, to function otherwise, to deliberately endorse modes of inefficiency, carelessness, and debt violates the norms of developed practical intelligence. Factory workers are men and women with hopes and dreams and aspirations; they have families, lovers, friends, and companions. They seek ways to develop and enhance their intellectual and creative potential. These men and women read (and sometimes write) books; they question their lives and labor. They seek ways to constitute themselves as attentive, inquiring, intelligent, reasonable, responsible, loving persons and to so constitute their society. Workers yearn for a standard of living that allows them to nourish the mind and spirit in dignity. They want the workplace ordered in such a way that their persons are honored. As we shall see, disregard for these standards has become endemic in the factory.

With the labor shortages of the Second World War, the automobile companies hired blacks in large numbers for the first time. "Chrysler's number of black women employees went from zero in 1941 to 5,000 by 1945."[50] The exception was Ford, although Ford used blacks as strike breakers for anti-union campaigns. The automobile companies cultivated and institutionalized group bias in the form of racism for their advantage. For example, at Chrysler's Dodge Main: "99 percent of all general foremen were white, 95 percent of all foremen were white, 100 percent of all superintendents were white, 90 percent of all skilled tradesmen were white, and 90 percent of all skilled apprentices."[51] In general, black and Arab workers were assigned the dirtiest, the noisiest, and the most dangerous jobs in the foundry, body shop, and engine assembly areas. These jobs required the greatest physical strain and exposed workers to poisonous combinations of chemicals and gases.[52]

Safety is a central feature of ordering factory work conditions and an index of regard for human life. But as Dan Georgakas and Marvin Surkin report in their analysis of the relations that structure a factory, health and accident data on the automobile industry have been difficult to obtain. Only since the early 1970s did the UAW and the Department of Health, Education and Welfare begin to conduct such studies. Georgakas and Surkin call attention to a pioneering study, *Health Research Group Study of Disease among Workers in the Auto Industry*, prepared in 1973 by two physicians, Jannette Sherman and Sidney Wolfe. Basing their findings on statistical evidence acquired from the National Institute of Occupational Safety and Health, Sherman and Wolfe made the following estimates:

> Sixty-five on-the-job deaths per day among auto workers, for a total of some 16,000 annually. Approximately half of these deaths were from heart attacks. There were also some 63,000 cases of disabling diseases and about 1,700,000 cases of lost or impaired hearing. These statistics did not include many long-term illnesses endemic to foundry workers and others exposed to poisonous chemicals and gases, nor did they include deaths and injuries by accident. Even these limited figures made it clear that more auto workers were killed and injured each year on the job than soldiers were killed and injured during any year of the war in Vietnam.[53]

Georgakas and Surkin record the painful disregard for worker safety in the name of higher productivity at a Chrysler Corporation five-plant cluster: Eldon Avenue Gear and Axle, Huber Foundry, Winfield Foundry, Chrysler Forge, and Plymouth. The Eldon plant was key to Chrysler operations. Corporation officials described the plant in a report to the National Labor Relations Board on November 30, 1971, as "engaged primarily in machining metal parts for rear axles of most Chrysler-built automobiles, for which it is the *sole* source, and assembling the parts into completed axles."[54] The Eldon plant covered one million square feet and included another half-million square feet of storage; it contained 2,600 machine tools of 170 different types. And Eldon employed a workforce of over 4,000, 70 percent of whom were black. Bitterly mocking the company's boast of automation, black workers considered those speedup methods "niggermation" and the Eldon plant "the most niggermated factory in Detroit."[55]

Despite its key role in Chrysler's operation, working conditions at Eldon continually diminished and demeaned the workers. Sexual harassment, physical intimidation of black and Arab workers by white foremen and white workers, industrial illnesses, injuries, and deaths on the job pushed Eldon workers beyond endurance.

There is the story of Mamie Williams, a fifty-one-year-old black woman who had worked for Chrysler for over twenty-six years.

> Mamie Williams had been ordered by her doctors to stay home because of a dangerous blood-pressure condition. Chrysler, however, had sent her a telegram telling her to return to work or be fired and lose all the benefits she had accumulated in almost three decades of employment. An intimidated Mamie Williams had returned to her job on the first shift in Department 80. One week later, she passed out on the line and died shortly after being taken home.[56]

There is the story of Rose Logan, a black janitor.

> Rose Logan had been struck in the plant by an improperly loaded jitney whose driver's vision was blocked. Her doctor told her to stay off her feet, but Chrysler's doctors ordered her back to work. She returned to Eldon from fear of losing her job, developed thrombophlebitis in her leg [and died].[57]

Then there is the story of John Taylor, a white worker, who writes:

> I worked on what they called a modern grinder. We used to laugh about it because there was nothing modern about it at all. It was ancient. We had to burn off the rough edges of rangers which looked like donuts with metal teeth. This part went into the differential. There was a lot of fine dust generated by this grinding. The company put vents on the machines to hold this down, but every shift the filters would get clogged. The supervisor would never give us the little time needed for someone to come and do some maintenance on them. I requested a mask. I got this thing that didn't look right and asked for the box it came in. It turned out to be for paint and gas fumes and was no help against dust. I ran all this down to McKinnon [the Union Steward in Department 75], but he refused to deal with it.[58]

Eldon's conditions were typical for the industry. Listen to Denise Stevenson:

> I work at a small shop in Troy. . . .Three weeks ago a woman on the day shift got her arm chopped off in a press. The week before this happened, the press repeated and they said they'd fixed it and kept people working on it and then this lady got her arm chopped off. People were really freaked out; some of the people on days ended up quitting.[59]

At the Eldon plant, the death of a twenty-two-year-old black worker, Gary Thompson, a former Vietnam veteran who was crushed under five tons of steel when the defective jitney he was driving overturned, forced the UAW safety director to investigate. Lloyd Utter sent an official interoffice communication to the assistant director of the National Chrysler Department.

> I examined the equipment and found the emergency brake to be broken; as a matter of fact, it was never connected. The shifter lever to the transmission was loose and sloppy. The equipment generally was sadly in need of maintenance, having lost the steering wheel in addition to other general needs. I also visited the repair area and observed other industrial trucks in this area that were sadly in need of repair, noting no lights, lack of brakes, horns, broken LP gas tank fasteners, loose steering wheels, leaky hydraulic equipment, etc. I was informed that there is supposed to be a regularly scheduled maintenance procedure for this equipment in this plant. I was also informed that operators are instructed to take trucks to the garage and tag them when they are in need of repairs. However, it seems to be the practice of foremen, when equipment is needed, to pull tags off the equipment in the repair area that badly need corrective maintenance and put them back into service on the floor. . . . Finally, a general observation as we passed to and from the location of the fatal accident: there seemed to be little attempt to maintain proper housekeeping except on the main front aisle. Water and grease were observed all along the way, as we proceeded. Every good safety program has its basic good-housekeeping procedures. Proper steps should be taken immediately to improve conditions within this plant.[60]

Is it any wonder that workers, especially men and women of color, see themselves as held in contempt by culture and society? Is it any wonder that workers often despise and abuse themselves and each other? Is it any wonder that these men and women suffer physical and psychological disabilities? Is it any wonder that their families suffer as well? Is it any wonder that resentment poisons the minds and hearts of so many men and women who work in factories?

Is such disregard and exploitation necessary in the workplace at all? While the factory cannot operate (practically and intelligently) at a loss, surely it can operate humanely. It is futile to badger the factory owner or chief operating officer or manager with vague moral precepts that merely censure greed. For any moral appeal to be effective, it must be appraised in the light of sound economic principles that address the concrete situation and the resultant implications of change—for the short and long terms. What is called for is not some mere patching and manipulative rearranging, but concrete change that is the result of thorough, rigorous, and detached study and evaluation. Yet the progress of any city— indeed, the progress of society and history—can never be realized solely through the concrete transformation of the conditions of the economic or political life. Most fundamentally what is required is the development of the intellectual, psychic, and moral capacities of women and men to face this decline and contest it. There is no substitute for the development of intelligent and responsible women and men. In the search for the right way to live, there is no substitute for the cultivation and nurturance of virtuous women and men who are able to reflect upon and to criticize human life and human history, who desire and seek the good, who choose wisely, who act justly, who love mercy, who walk humbly with God (Micah 6:8).

Unions, Values, and Skills
Richard Barnet and Ronald Müller identify the crisis of the American labor movement as "a fundamental crisis of human obsolescence."[61] On two counts this characterization is correct. First, the authors correlate the American worker's dwindling role in the global reorganization of production to the wages the U.S. standard of living requires, and to the corporate practice of avoiding labor tensions by automating and/or transferring production to under-developed

countries. Further, Barnet and Müller connect these features to increased structural unemployment, for, as modern capitalist society defines work, there is less and less for men and women to do in the production process.[62] Second, Barnet and Müller show how these problems contribute to worker alienation. "The byproduct of efficiency and increased productivity is the superfluous man whose only social function is to consume."[63] Workers feel "that industrial society has left them with the dull, hard, dirty jobs—and doesn't care."[64] Union officials themselves, "aware that the humanization of work opens up issues of industrial relations far tougher and deeper than the traditional trade-union demands on which labor-bureaucrats have built their power, are skittish about the subject."[65] These officials suspect (and rightly) that reorganization of the workplace might lead to the reorganization of unions themselves.[66]

Detroit, its people, its vital social (technological, economic, political) and cultural health continually dangle between industry and union: both want to make cars at a profit, both opt for short-term common-sense solutions, both fail to calculate the long-term consequences—not merely the social (technological, economic, and political) consequences, but the cultural and personal consequences. When union negotiators fail to perceive that collective bargaining is really about human dignity, about a standard of living that preserves, enhances, and realizes instances of true value, they betray the men and women whom they represent. Being human is more than having a bundle of desires; there is much more to life than mere consumption. Barnet and Müller quite bluntly state that the problems workers face will not be solved by turning "the superfluous, nonverbal worker of average intelligence into a pensioner by means of a guaranteed annual income or, as some have suggested, to award him an annual 'consumer in residence' grant."[67]

Displaying their own biased brand of common sense, union leaders perceive problems in the factory solely as external; hence they pose externalized solutions. Progress is correlated with material possessions. The good that is pursued in union-management bargaining is the good as experienced; the good as intelligible, as reasonable, as a concrete expression of true value is ignored. The exercise of power (through the strike or walkout; through the lockout or automation) and resentful responses to whoever has seized the upper hand replace human fellow-feeling in pursuit of a worthwhile aim. Thus, the social order is grasped as a result of power relations, and intelligence, regard, and esteem are increasingly irrelevant to "things as they are" in that order.

Workers speak frequently of societal disdain for their skills and for them, of their lack of autonomy and control over their lives, of their powerlessness in the workplace, of their resignation to economic circumstances and their implications. And they speak of the continual effacement of human dignity that leaves them with feelings of personal inadequacy and meaninglessness.[68]

> The feelings of injured dignity come not only from the meaninglessness of work but from the prevailing social climate which disparages manual labor and grants prestige only to marketable intellectual skills. The [high-school] education for which their parents sacrificed, which was supposed to have brought freedom, has turned out to be the entrance requirement for a boring job.[69]

Factory workers long for more than increased wages: they long for signs and symbols of respect and courtesy, for a share in the ordering of the workplace, for opportunities to exercise creativity and freedom, for recognition of themselves as persons.[70]

At the same time, factory workers have embraced material possessions as badges of success, as rewards (or entitlements) for enduring the indignities of the factory. However, with widespread automation, there is little incentive to utilize the walkout or the strike; workers have become preoccupied with protecting their material goods. Here we meet one of the contradictions of the current way in which the economic order is structured and intertwined with the political order. Here we see the power of the technological order over the economy and the polity. James Boggs, a factory worker, calls for creative criticism of this subordination of the political order to the economic and technological orders. He challenges workers to think and act imaginatively and creatively, to go beyond the realm of the material. Boggs contends that the "greatest human need in the United States today" is the need "to stop shirking responsibility and start assuming responsibility."[71] He knows that factory workers need and long for more than bread, and so, in a nondominating way, he urges them to take their lives seriously—to begin the arduous and fulfilling process of self-transformation, of living intelligently and creatively.[72] Moreover, by insisting on critical, intelligent, and creative engagement with the social order, Boggs pushes beyond the common-sense view of human responsibility for that order and of our roles within it. His position is compatible with Lonergan's radical invitation to a "self-appropriation which cognitively, morally, and religiously respects and seeks to promote effective human freedom."[73]

The Transcendent Solution

In the concluding pages of *Insight,* Lonergan reformulates the idea of progress. To resist decline, we must develop in our attentiveness to experience, in our understanding of the concrete human situation, in our ability to judge reasonably; we must do what is good and right in response to the human situation. This development in knowing and doing, the appropriation and concrete realization of rational self-consciousness, is the means by which we men and women can take intelligent control of our social world, of history, of the realization of human good.

Yet that control is flawed—and not only control of that social world: we women and men limp in the disequilibrium of our own moral impotence. Complete self-development and practical realization of that development in society are long and difficult processes. There is a gap between the conditioned effective freedom that a man or a woman possesses and the hypothetical freedom he or she would have if conditions were otherwise. Our awareness of our own moral impotence heightens the tension between the limitations of who we happen to be (conditioned by external circumstances, our psychic and intellectual development, and our decisions and actions) and the transcending thrust toward who we are to be. But these insights on our moral selves are ambiguous. On the one hand, they are lessons in humility, reminders that our living is a developing and that we may profit from failure; on the other hand, they can be regarded as evidence by which to lower our moral horizon and to rest content with ourselves as we are.[74] We have seen how the consequences of this gap in our knowing and doing spills over into concrete institutions of the social order. The factory and the condition of workers reflect our failure in converted human living. This and other such breakdowns result from decisions and living that diverge from the immanent norms of developed intelligence and its correlative action. And once the surd "penetrates and pervades the cultural dimension of society," once the surd characterizes the cultural dimension of society, moral impotence becomes quite commonplace and the history which we forge "closes in to become, not a thrust toward God, but a reign of sin."[75]

There is a higher-order integration of the concrete universal that is man and there is an absolutely supernatural solution to the fact of individual and social evil. Added to the biological, psychic, and intellectual levels of development is a fourth level that includes "the higher conjugate forms of faith, hope, and charity" which, in themselves, "constitute an absolutely supernatural living that advances toward an absolutely supernatural goal under the action of divine grace."[76] This solution as a higher integration of human living is a "harmonious continuation of the actual order of the universe," which is a "good and value chosen by God." This solution proceeds along the lines of emergent probability but under the stimulus of an act of divine grace that respects human freedom. Thus, as a higher integration, this solution is carried out in the exercise of human intelligence, in cooperation with the gifts of faith, hope, and charity that suffuse sensitive psychic and intersubjective development. In discerning and carrying out that solution, human intelligence must grasp that the "social surd neither is intelligible nor is to be treated as intelligible"; correspondingly, the will grasps that evil is to be met with good. The social surd becomes a potential good as men and women meet evil with good, love their enemies, and pray for those who persecute and oppress them. Expressed compactly and symbolically, the transcendent solution to the problem of evil is the passion, death, and resurrection of Jesus of Nazareth who is the

Christ.[77] Such love absorbs the surd of sin and breaks the cycle of decline that obstructs the concrete realization of the human good in society and history.

A Concluding Theology of Social Transformation

To repeat, theology can in no way substitute for the human and social sciences; yet these sciences can become practical only through theology. Thus, a politically responsible and methodical theology of social transformation collaborates actively with the human and social sciences in efforts to apprehend, understand, and diagnose the human condition. Indeed, such a theology is attuned to the voices and discourses that emerge among marginated women and men of various racial, ethnic-cultural, and economic communities. It is attuned to the angry and implosive cry of the underclass;[78] to the agony of men, women, and children with AIDS;[79] to the anguish of the homeless; to the heartache of women and children living on subsistence; to the despair of men and women who are incarcerated not only in prisons but in massive poverty, illiteracy, ignorance, and self-hatred. A politically responsible methodical theology of social transformation brings to anthropology and cultural studies, to sociology and psychology, to political and economic inquiry, this reminder: these concrete men and women cannot be reduced to statistics or illustrations of this or that sociological or economic or psychological problem or theory. Such a theology stands as a higher viewpoint that reinforces the social scientist's detached and disinterested desire to know; it urges the social scientist to seek practically intelligent, reasonable, and responsible solutions to human problems. Moreover, it invites the social scientist to place her or his intellectual efforts at the service of the progress of the common human good, to persevere in the search for responsible, creative, and healing solutions to those problems, especially when the situation is most opaque. For a politically responsible theology of social transformation regards men and women as persons—flawed, struggling creatures yearning for

God—capable of understanding, of conscious and intentional decision-making, of transformed and responsible living, of converted relationships. For these men and women of this concrete world are conditioned by sin and by whether they accept or refuse God's gift of grace. And the human good is contingent upon the fostering, nurturing, and sustaining of authentic human personhood through the transformations of religious, moral, and intellectual conversion; upon the critical and conscientious scrutiny of the complex recurrent schemes and relations that bring about a beautiful order of living; and upon those judgments of value realized in human practice.

A theology of social transformation stimulates, among various groups and individuals, serious grappling with questions that shape critical, creative, and responsible living. Do I know what it means to make my own decisions? Do I know what I am making of myself in my daily choices and refusals? Do I understand that my liberty is the very delicate and fragile possibility of orienting myself in life for eternal life? Do I know what it means to respect others, to be in love with them? Do I know what it means to be a human person? Under what cultural and social (political, economic, and technological) conditions can human beings be truly and fully human persons? As I strive to answer that question, do I sufficiently grasp that the conditions for human flourishing are the results of acts of human judgment and decision? Do I sufficiently grasp that the conditions for human flourishing are not something extrinsic, something prefabricated, something already-out-there-now? As I strive to find ways to promote and expand the conditions for human flourishing, how can I encourage and support the efforts of detached and disinterested intelligence without those very efforts succumbing to bias? What conjunction of values and practical intelligence promotes authentic progress? Have I anticipated concretely just what self-transcending love might mean in the effort to overcome decline? Do I know what it means to suffer? Do I know what it means to know, to live, to value, to love in the presence of God?

By struggling and sharing in the struggle with such questions, the theologian exposes the poverty as well as the potential of all human efforts and solutions to meet the problem of evil. With such questions and their answers, a politically responsible methodical theology goes beyond partisan advocacy and offers a type of collaboration almost unimagined in current styles of political theology. With such questions and their answers, a politically responsible methodical theology contests the fragmentation and ideological conflict that inhibits us from grasping the intrinsic connections between life, the good life, and eternal life.

A just society (as evidence of the progress of the human good) is contingent. The lives, suffering, and deaths of Mamie Williams, Rose Logan, John Taylor, Denise Stevenson, and Gary Thompson testify to just how contingent it is. For a just society is contingent upon human acts of intelligence or obtuseness, of reasonableness or unreasonableness, of responsibility or irresponsibility. A just society is constituted by just men and women who so live that the truth, intelligibility, goodness, and beauty of the good of order are radiant. To be sure, a politically responsible methodical theology of social transformation criticizes and evaluates the progress—or the decline—of the social and cultural matrix. But it does more. Through inquiry into the relations, meanings, and values that constitute that matrix, such a theology finds concrete ways to collaborate in the creation of real possibilities that improve the odds of solving human problems. Moreover, such a theology recognizes that those solutions cannot be envisioned apart from the reign of sin or from the recovery offered by divine grace. For it is only through the gift of grace realized in human lives and hearts that our values and practices can meet the effects of sin that vitiate the social order, that spawn the crisis of the human good.

3
Tasting the Bitter with the Sweet
The Spiritual Geography of Newark, New Jersey
Linda Mercadante

Newark, New Jersey, has taken a bad rap for years. Only ten miles west of New York City, it is a place many people know only in passing. For some, the closest they have been to Newark is the ugly stretch of the New Jersey Turnpike they drive on their way between Manhattan and Philadelphia. For many people in the Northeast, not just Newark but all of New Jersey is just a corridor—a place analogous to the Midwest, which is often dismissed by residents of both coasts as the "flyover zone." Adding insult to this, New Jersey has long been the punch line of jokes, the place where residents are supposed to identify each other simply by asking, "What exit?"

If New Jersey is the butt of jokes, some visualize Newark as the burned core, perhaps best known in the twentieth century for its 1967 race riots. There is some justification for the stereotypical disparagement of Newark. The riots came at a particularly bad time, for Newark—like many other U.S. cities—had long been racked by city hall corruption, deserted by many for the suburbs, and was overbuilt with public housing. Thirty years after the riots, in spite of gallant efforts at revitalization, Newark was declared the most dangerous city in America. Since the city is geographically small (only about twenty-six square miles) relative to its large population (some 273,546 in 2000), crowding has been a problem. Thus, although Newark has welcomed newcomers throughout its history, it has also been a revolving door, the place that people aspire to leave. Finally, Newark struggles financially, especially as 75 percent of its economic base is made up of institutions and services that are non-tax-paying.[1]

Yet this largest city in New Jersey has a proud history. The land that became Newark was purchased in 1666 from the Hackensack Indians by several Puritan families from Connecticut and originally named Milford. In 1747 the College of New Jersey, which became Princeton University, was established there, and in 1776 Washington's army marched through it. It is the third-oldest major city (after Boston and New York) in the United States, officially chartered in 1836. Newark has long given immigrants a place to start, originally welcoming English, German, Scottish, and Irish. By the turn of the century, the city housed the nation's fifth-largest Italian community.[2] The city has also been home to many African Americans, and at least since the 1950s, they have been the majority group. Representative of this, in 1970 Newark elected the first black mayor of a major eastern city, Kenneth Gibson.

This ethnic and cultural diversity continues into the present and is a source of pride. Newark is situated in a state that is first in the nation in the variety of its immigrant population—and known for its liberal attitudes toward them.[3] Over time, Newark has birthed a many-hued medley of cultural heroes, including Stephen Crane, Aaron Burr, Sarah Vaughan, Whitney Houston, Connie Francis, Philip Roth, Imamu Amiri Baraka, Shaquille O'Neal, and Queen Latifah. Today the city is home to a vibrant enclave of Portuguese and Brazilian immigrants, as well many other Hispanics from Puerto Rico, the Caribbean, and elsewhere in Latin America. In fact, there are at least a dozen Spanish-speaking communities in the city.

Additionally, Newark carries on the tradition that began in the nineteenth century, when it was one of the first three manufacturing cities in the United States and the site of many inventions, including plastic, patent leather, malleable iron, and air conditioning. Today it is still the site of successful industries and the home base of the Prudential insurance company. The city also houses five institutions of higher learning and an impressive performing arts center. It has a good public library system and several excellent museums. The reality, then, is not as negative as the stereotype.[4] Newark, like many other older cities in America, has much to offer and can inspire loyalty, even fondness, from its residents.

Nevertheless, Newark is like many other places that are not on the "most desirable" list for mobile Americans. Life there, as in many urban locales, is bittersweet. While residents can develop an understandable attachment to the "hood" that isn't simply the by-product of limited vision and deprivation, Newark is also a place many residents hope someday to leave. The sweetness of authentic belonging mixes with a bitter and an ineffable longing, born of deprivation and desire, that eventually impels flight. In this bittersweet life, the two tastes so intermingle that it is hard to tell them apart.

On Location in Newark

I was born and raised in Newark and lived above my family's Italian-American pastry shop on busy Bloomfield Avenue. In an inadvertent, almost Forrest Gump–like fashion, I found myself involved in many crucial moments during an eventful period in Newark's history. Two pivotal events accompanied my beginnings and indelibly marked me. Both occurred just a few blocks from where we lived. In 1953 the vibrant Italian-American First Ward—Newark's half-century-old Little Italy and the most prominent of the city's four such areas—was razed in a misguided attempt at urban renewal. I grew up hearing older Italian Americans talk wistfully about the joys of that neighborhood where everyone knew everyone and felt part of an extended family. In the same breath, they would also talk bitterly of the eight twelve-story low-income projects, the "Columbus Homes," that replaced it. These forbidding-looking structures went downhill quickly. I was around in the 1970s when they were declared as big a failure as the Pruitt-Igo homes in St. Louis. But the hulks remained to haunt the area until 1994, when they were imploded.

The other event stood in complete contrast. In 1954 Sacred Heart Cathedral—a French Gothic–style treasure patterned after Rheims, about the same size as England's Westminster Cathedral and taller than Notre Dame in Paris—was dedicated after nearly a hundred years in the works. It soon took its place as the pride of area Roman Catholics and as a revered city landmark. As a testament to the power of worship space, it was to have a lasting effect on the spiritual formation of many in the area, including myself. Both events testify to the profound force that environment and architecture exert on spirit.

Other crucial episodes in this city also marked my experience of it. In 1967, as a young student, I took a summer job downtown at Blue Cross–Blue Shield and thus witnessed the Newark riots firsthand. With a National Guard encampment at Newark Schools Stadium just down the street from our business and apartment, we daily witnessed military vehicles rolling by to handle the violence downtown. Several times I crouched on the floor of our living room, peering out the windows at vigilante cars passing with rifles sticking out the windows.

When urban decline made it harder to keep our business going, my parents rented a street-level section of our building to neighborhood son Anthony Imperiale. The space, directly below my third-floor bedroom, was used for about a year as his political office until a brick crashed through our storefront, the rent went unpaid, and my parents realized the situation was not viable. Imperiale for years was a real presence in Newark. He had reached national prominence during the period of racial unrest, vowing to defend his neighborhood at all costs.

In 1972, as a young newspaper reporter, I covered the pickets and protests over plans to build a residential high-rise, the Kawaida Towers, in a Hispanic, African, and Italian American single-family-home neighborhood along Mt. Prospect Avenue. A project of African American religious leader Imamu Amiri Baraka (once also a poet known as LeRoi Jones), he and Imperiale kept the press busy daily as they fought bitterly over the issues. In my interviews with the principals and residents in this dispute, I learned that what looked like a simple case of black versus white was actually much more complex, having to do with ethnicity and the tenuous achievements of poor and lower-middle-class people.

Much of this took place on or near Bloomfield Avenue. This historic thoroughfare was originally an old Indian trail and opened in 1809 as an 11.2-mile toll road named the Newark and Pompton Turnpike. As the state's first county route, it has long been the main artery connecting seven northern New Jersey towns. It begins near one of the oldest sections of Newark, nearly downtown, and goes all the way to the upscale Caldwells.[5] Most of Bloomfield Avenue is lined with small businesses, many with apartments above, and some single-family homes. Think of the opening shots in the HBO television series *The Sopranos,* as Tony exits the highway and drives home, with buildings spacing out and getting larger as he drives north, and you've got a good picture of its character.

The traffic on Bloomfield Avenue was a clear indicator of "white flight." Since my bedroom on the third floor of our building faced this street, each morning I would hear and smell the heavy traffic heading from the suburbs toward downtown, and each afternoon watch these same people depart. Being allowed to cross this busy street by ourselves was a major rite of passage for myself, my brother and my two cousins, since all of us lived in our parents' two apartments above the bakery, and we played on the sidewalk in front. My family's living room also faced this street, and during the week, large trucks going by would make it impossible to hear the dialogue on our television. The quiet of Sunday afternoon, when suburbanites stayed home, seemed deadly eerie by contrast.

I was never sure whether I felt at home in Newark or hated it. Usually I felt both at the same time. The ethnic community, our business, the closeness of family members, the good food and easy transportation vied in my psyche with the lack of space, little accessible vegetation, restricted social roles, the ever-present sense of danger, and the humiliation of living in a place that people always made fun of. This bittersweet background—and the sense of both belonging there and yet longing for more—is what I take from my time in Newark. Although I cannot speak for all urban residents, I believe that my experience there offers a microcosmic sampling of a city's spiritual geography, showing what gives life and what takes it away in a place like Newark.

The Bitter

It's hard to live in a state that is the butt of jokes. I don't know when this started. But at least by the late 1950s, television comics from New York played mercilessly with New Jersey's reputation. And even in everyday life, New Jerseyans, upon identifying themselves, were often greeted with "Oh, you live in *Joisey*," the fake accent accompanied with a smirk. Specific cities in New Jersey share an even worse reputation. Newark, in the public mind, is ranked alongside or perhaps below the also lambasted Jersey City.[6] When I identified my birthplace as Newark, even state residents often treated this revelation with condescension, pity, or outright disgust. It was a real conversation-stopper.

By the 1960s, Newark had lost most of its once-prominent Jewish population. Although this trend had started in the 1930s, as residents sought better education for their children, it was finalized when the construction of Route 78 literally cut the historically Jewish Weequahic section in half. By then Newark was also rapidly losing much of its middle class in general. Because of its small size, as the city grew, people moved farther out. Once public transportation—first trolleys and buses, then the automobile and road construction—made commuting feasible, people who could afford it began moving out of Newark. In this part of northern New Jersey, towns are contiguous and distances relatively short, so it was quite possible to live in a quiet suburb and still work in Newark.

It seemed for my family, however, that because of our business, we were stuck in Newark. I can still hear my mother impatiently saying to a telephoning customer that, yes, the bakery is still located here in Newark and, yes, it is safe to come down here to shop. Once, after yet another customer—one of many who had left the neighborhood but still hankered after decent cannoli—

demanded that we deliver her order because she was afraid to drive there, my mother said with exasperation: "What do you think *I* am, chopped liver? We *live* here."

Ours was not a unique experience. Urban residents who cannot or do not choose to leave, often feel abandoned and betrayed—and with good reason. The North Ward, where we lived, is a case in point. It had first been eviscerated by the razing of Newark's First Ward, the proud ethnic community that had seen the likes of Joe DiMaggio, Billie Holiday, Jayne Mansfield, and Frank Sinatra in its establishments. The area had less than fifteen years to adjust—a period during which the city was suffering increased middle-class flight, corruption, and mismanaged finances—when the riots erupted in nearby downtown, prompting more desertions. Only a few years later the attempt to plant Kawaida Towers in the Ward further demoralized and confused the neighborhood.

Today only parts of the Italian American community remain. There is no going back to the family feeling that existed for former residents of the Ward. From the 1870s, when the first Italians arrived in Newark, to its heyday from about 1880 to 1925, this area was the most densely populated Italian neighborhood in Newark, with over 80 percent of its foreign-born from Italy. Although many struggled financially, the Ward's community feeling was legendary. It also served as a center of religious life, hosting many societies honoring saints. Along with many feasts and celebrations in the neighborhood, its most famous ethnic church, St. Lucy's, was home to the widely celebrated St. Gerard Maiella festival each October.

Urban renewal changed much of that. Thousands of residents, both Italian and African American, were dislocated, and most of them did not return. Fortunately, St. Lucy's bravely fought to remain standing during urban renewal, although the destruction sur-rounded it front and back. In 1977 the church was declared the national shrine of St. Gerard, and each year still hosts thousands of pilgrims. But annual pilgrimage does not make up for the wistful longing that the displaced residents and descendants of the area inchoately feel. Therefore, while places like the North Ward legiti-mately serve as staging areas and jumping-off points for immigrants, in this case, many of the changes were beyond residents' control.

Only recently has the site of the imploded Columbus Homes been filled by several successful and handsome low-rise housing developments. This is nearly fifty years after the First Ward was razed. Fortunately, the current North Ward, home to over 55,000, is still vital. Recently a small number of professional people, many of whom make the relatively easy commute to Manhattan, have begun moving there. Primarily the neighborhood is Hispanic, along with the African American community that has always been a part of the area. Today on Bloomfield Avenue many of the Italian store signs have been replaced by Spanish ones, as life along the avenue goes on.

Recently I visited there. Our bakery has been replaced by a laundromat. The Spanish-speaking manager graciously showed me how they had retrofitted the place to house his apartment in back where the ovens used to be, and how the many washing machines and dryers had been installed in front where once pastries were displayed and sold. It was disorienting to see this place so changed—it had been the anchor of my whole reality growing up. Yet I did feel comfortable being back in the neighborhood. My young son, however, who accompanied me, did not. He felt all eyes were upon us, for we were now just some of those who stay briefly and then drive away. We had lunch in the shop of an elderly pizza man, one of the Italian stragglers. He spoke with gloom about changes in the neighborhood and seemed worn down by the struggle of ensuring his financial, emotional, and physical well-being. But he was impressed that I had gotten out and even become a professor. I felt ashamed at having deserted.

As we walked around, I noted that the character of the place had not changed. The crowding, crumbling buildings, graffiti-laden walls, worn pavement, and lack of greenery reminded me why I had wanted so badly to leave. Today the sidewalk along Bloomfield Avenue sports some struggling little trees, but they are not nearly enough to challenge the heat, dirt, and hardness of miles of cement and asphalt. This was the first time my son had ever seen this place. His appalled reaction highlighted how different my childhood was from the suburban reality that is his.

It would take a trained and accustomed eye to see much of the beauty in Newark, but some of it is more obvious. Only several blocks from our former building is the ward's Forest Hill section, still proud with large homes and older trees. Although many of these homes are now used as multi-family dwellings, the neighborhood still contains some of the prime residential property in the city. Contiguous to this is the magnificent Branch Brook Park. As the first Essex County park, it began with 60 acres in 1895, designed by Frederick Law Olmsted's firm, also responsible for Manhattan's Central Park. Now nearly 500 acres, this Newark park is the site of between 2,000 and 3,000 ornamental cherry trees of four different species—the world's largest collection, larger even than that in Washington, D.C.—with its own Cherry Blossom Festival each April.[7]

It is not an unalloyed grace, however. Like many urban parks, it can suffer from problems such as litter and vandalizing. And although it is used by tens of thousands of people yearly, I remember neighborhood families considering the park dangerous. While its winding roads and ample trees make it known as the "lungs of Essex County," in my experience, many area children only observed it from a passing bus or car. I found it discouraging to have such beauty inaccessible.

The North Ward of Newark, then, aptly demonstrates many of the bitter pills city residents must swallow. Shame, abandonment, despair, like poison gases, are silently emitted by the urban environment. One's sense of home, place, and self is permeated by many difficult feelings and realities. There is the worry that one's neighbors will desert the area at first opportunity. As different waves of immigrants and ethnic groups replace each other, longtime inhabitants can feel increasingly out of place. As I interviewed some of those who remain, I sensed a defensive tone.

Urban residents may see around them reduced job prospects and feel further betrayed if their area is on the short end of the stick for public monies. There is a vague but ever-present threat of danger. Personal space is at a minimum compared with the suburbs, and the hard surfaces and resultant temperature extremes make life uncomfortable. It is often difficult (whether financially or logistically) to add modern conveniences. On top of all this, one cannot help but recognize that one is out of step with the "normal" lifestyle as seen on television and in film and magazines. To this add parents' concerns that available schools are not necessarily safe or effective, that children have few open spaces to play in, and that if one's progeny become successful, they must move away. These all contribute to a bitterness in urban life, even if one lives in a relatively vigorous neighborhood like Newark's North Ward and can manage to attain a lower-middle-class lifestyle. It is no wonder that many urban dwellers of cities like Newark harbor a deep sense of shame, no matter how well covered up by bravado, resourcefulness, energy, and anger.

After years of popular psychologizing, we know that shame is a spiritual cancer. It eats away at one's self-esteem, sense of identity, and relationship with others. This sense of being a nobody from nowhere with no hope can propel people to do things and react in ways that are self-destructive, counterproductive, and aggressive. The first hope I had that the gospel might be meaningful for me personally is when I heard that Jesus, too, had to deal with less-than-auspicious origins. When onlookers asked disparagingly about him, "What good can come out of Nazareth?" I knew what they meant and I felt a sense of connection.

The Sweet

But there is also much that is sweet in a city like Newark. In older neighborhoods like the North Ward, buildings usually do not dwarf humans. Single- and multiple-family dwellings, smaller apartment buildings, units above shops—all give a person a chance to emotionally carve out a space and get to know the nearby inhabitants. Life seems more manageable when you know the personalities and idiosyncracies of your neighbors. If there is a problem, at least you may discover its source and know that it is likely experienced by others as well. Cooperation benefits everyone. If hallways, entrances, drives, or sidewalks are regularly shared, it is not as easy to draw a cloak of anonymity and its partner, loneliness, around you. Interdependency may slow down productivity sometimes, but the synergy of human interaction can also bring about unexpected joys.

We were fortunate on Bloomfield Avenue to have diverse businesses that took care of many aspects of daily life. Within a four-block radius were numerous small food stores, a shoe repair shop, a tailor, several pharmacies, a toy store, a variety store, several restaurants, taverns, pizza places, and bakeries, as well as two banks, some social clubs, insurance agencies, a public garage, and a gas station. Although shops occasionally changed owners or were replaced with other businesses, there was a continuity in the variety offered. Store owners got to know the people in the neighborhood, shopping was a social event, and it was fairly safe to send children on errands. This made for a rich environment for everyone.

My brother used to hang out at the cobbler's next door, remembering fondly how he was allowed to pound in nails. I used to visit the men's store that rented space in my family's building. The genial owner made me feel important because he listened to me. The butcher down the street knew what kind of meat my parents wanted, so even as a little girl I could go there alone. This gave me a sense of responsibility and freedom. While these types of experiences are not as likely in mall America, they are still possible anywhere small businesses and a sense of mutuality exist in a neighborhood. Being able to do errands in one's own neighborhood, especially on foot, makes life more whole. The young, the handicapped, and the elderly, then, are not as easily cut out of normal life or made overly dependent upon others. Exercise, human interaction, and taking care of business all happen at the same time for a wider range of people.

This small scale and everyday familiarity can also cushion the sense of danger that urban dwellers often have. This was a mixed blessing in my neighborhood. What feels like self-determination and protection to residents can be experienced as intolerance by others. America first heard of Anthony Imperiale in 1967 when racial tensions erupted in Newark. Conducting street patrols and vowing to defend his neighborhood with a baseball bat if necessary, Imperiale became a national symbol of white backlash. But locally Imperiale was respected as a former Marine, Korean War veteran, and karate teacher who organized a volunteer emergency squad that served everyone in the neighborhood regardless of race. Residents also appreciated his sense of humor. He was a fixture in Newark's Columbus Day parades, amusing spectators by dressing in outlandish outfits, one year going as a gladiator and sharing his float with a live lion.

For some locals, Imperiale's community service balanced out his opposition to school busing during the early 1960s and his rhetoric during the 1967 riots and the Kawaida Towers debacle. Although many feared him, he was able to build on the neighborhood's mutual-aid principle successfully enough to launch an impressive political career.[8] For all the controversy inspired by Imperiale, clearly residents approved of his desire to protect the North Ward and Newark.

But urban danger can also be averted through the anonymous spiritual guardians of a neighborhood. In the Bronx where some of my other relatives lived, it was Jewish grandmothers leaning out their tenement windows observing street life. During my time in the North Ward, it was the Italian widows in their black dresses food shopping for their extended households but focusing a keen eye on things, or it was the old men sitting outside social clubs or playing bocce ball in the park. A few blocks away, it was the African American mothers monitoring the neighborhood parks and apartment hallways.

Thus, the human scale, accessibility of services, and vibrant presence of people on the street were all important factors in nurturing life in Newark when I lived there. In addition, the architecture itself sweetened life and inspired spirits. While there are many attractive residences in the Ward, as well as older buildings lending a cozy air with the warmth of ruddy brick and ironwork, there are two places in particular that have been key for the area: the Clark mansion and the Sacred Heart Cathedral. Although their uses have changed somewhat since they were formative for me, these two structures still inspire and aid residents today.

Environment for the Spirit:
The Clark Mansion and the Sacred Heart Cathedral
At 346 Mt. Prospect Avenue, in the Forest Hill section of the North Ward, stands an imposing twenty-eight-room Georgian-style

manor house. It began life in 1880, constructed for J. William Clark, founder of the Clark Thread Mills. The residence, designed by noted architect William Halsey Wood, was located in a sylvan area north of the city. Set on a hill, it had a fabulous view of the Manhattan skyline and the Passaic River valley. At the turn of the century, the home was considered one of the most handsome in the country. It was graced by a portico entrance, massive entry doors, carved wooden balustrades, stained glass, decorative ceilings, richly appointed fireplaces, and chandeliers. As the center of social life for the area, this residence was complete with ballroom, library, and manicured grounds. The home was inhabited by Clark until his death in 1902, then owned for a time by another prominent Newark family, the Hellers.

In 1925, the building was purchased for $100,000 by Prospect Hill Country Day School. The school, which had been in existence as early as 1875, had been located away from the urban bustle, thus its name. By mid-century the city had grown up around it. Nevertheless, still surrounded by the one wooded acre left from the many it had previously owned (and eventually ceded to Branch Brook Park), it retained a spacious feeling. Educating children from kindergarten through high school—co-ed only through second grade—Prospect Hill became my school from seventh through ninth grades. I had previously attended public school, but my parents were determined I would be the first in our immediate family to attend college. They were thus like many others of immigrant roots who make financial sacrifices to improve their children's lot. Ultimately, my parents' plan worked, but it also set me on a trajectory that led away from Newark.

Although Prospect Hill was just a fifteen-minute walk from busy Bloomfield Avenue, to me the grounds and school felt like an entirely different world. The architecture and grace of the environment seemed to have a calming effect on me and my small class of young teenage girls. In the study hall, located in the old ballroom, I often stared at the ceiling and fireplace carvings, amazed that someone had taken the time to do this just for beauty. Light shone through the stained glass and played on the wooden carvings of the massive staircase that we took to get to our classrooms. It was an enchanting place and quite different from my usual world of asphalt, traffic, and cement.

The problem, however, was that some of us would never be able to replicate this environment. While there were many wealthy girls at Prospect Hill, I and my cousin, who was also a student there, did not come from such homes. Rather, we were the product of working-class parents who were determined to better the familial lot. As a twelve-year-old gazing at the woodwork and imagining gala evenings, I did not realize that in the early 1900s while wealthy guests were dancing here, my immigrant ancestors had been living in crowded substandard housing, working in sweatshops, and hoping to simply get by. But in some ways my ignorance was just as well. For this gracious environment seemed to give me an expanded vision for life, a love of beauty and learning, and a profound appreciation for the effect of surroundings on spirit.

The school closed in the 1970s, and the mansion stood vacant for a time. But in 1973 it found new life as the home of the North Ward Educational and Cultural Center. This organization, which still flourishes today, was founded by Stephen N. Adubato, an Italian American with a long lineage in the North Ward, and one of those who did not move after the riots. Adubato, who supported Gibson and was often at loggerheads with Imperiale, set up the organization in a storefront on Bloomfield Avenue shortly after the mayoral election. This native son's dedication to the area was similar to Imperiale's, but he had very different tactics. His group thus raised funds to purchase the mansion, and its new life began.

Although much of the home's architectural beauty had been retained throughout its history, a fire in 1976 prompted the new owners to do further restorations, which returned more of the mansion to its original appearance. Today this building is even more available to the public than it was as a girls' school. It seems that residents appreciate its presence, for little graffiti or trash mar its walls and grounds. Indeed, the nonprofit agency housed here is a key stabilizing force in the neighborhood. It has a $9 million yearly budget and provides job training, adult day care, preschool, transportation, recreation, and social services for the mostly Hispanic residents of the area. I imagine it also does for neighborhood people what it did for me—gives them a sense of beauty, pride, and a vision of how environment can affect attitude. And amazingly, a new and well-respected charter school has emerged in connection with the Center—the Robert Treat Academy—giving more than 250 area children expanded possibilities.

If the environment of Prospect Hill nurtured my intellect when I lived in Newark, Sacred Heart Cathedral spoke to my heart. Indeed, for many it was—and may still be—the heart of the neighborhood. It represents the funds and toil of locals, for although the stained glass was imported, its stone and wood work was done entirely by Newark artisans. Said to be the finest example of French Gothic architecture in the Western Hemisphere, in 1976 it was designated a national historic landmark, only one of three such churches in New Jersey. In 1995 Pope John Paul II presided there during a visit and elevated its status to a minor basilica, so it is now known as the Cathedral Basilica of the Sacred Heart.

Its location helps its aura. Set like a crown jewel at the head of Branch Brook park, the Cathedral has two towers that rise ten stories, making it visible from far away.[9] But although it is huge, it does not seem to dwarf human life, but to pick it up in an inclusive embrace toward God. The statuary, stained glass windows, many large side chapels, altars, and carvings speak of another dimension beyond what we can see. Added to this is masterful music on the immense organ, singing by trained choirs, and, during my time there, incense and Latin.

For me, the glory of this architecture wordlessly preached sermons that I remember far beyond what I may have heard from the pulpit. With eyes, ears, and nose enthralled, I found that my mind shifted gears and moved into a more liminal space. At the time, however, my spirit had to be nurtured passively. There was little room for me, both young and female, to participate in an authoritarian, male-dominated institution. Indeed, its American clerical structure wasn't an easy place even for priests of my own ethnic group to advance.[10] For someone drawn to the church, as I was, these layers of hierarchy meant that the imaginative place in my spirit was the main one in which I found freedom. Fortunately, the cathedral's environment nurtured that place.

In fact, I had quite a lot of mental and spiritual liberty. Since my parental home was nonreligious, I did not attend parochial school, and the nuns and priests paid little attention to me. With the beautiful but somewhat obscure Latin mass, the perfunctory homilies, and only minimal religious education, there was plenty of time to let the environment communicate grace and peace. Additionally, the opportunities and religious freedom of America meant I was not consigned to a passive role forever. But again, that freedom took me away from Newark. Eventually, pursuing knowledge, significant work, and a desire for a more active spirituality, I landed in mainline Protestantism. I found it intellectually satisfying and more accepting of women, but sensorily it felt minimalist, especially in comparison with my spiritual roots. While today I often mourn my geographic distance from the cathedral's spirit-birthing environment, this exceptional place in Newark is still there to nurture others.

Some Theological Dimensions of Environment

What can we make of all this theologically? I suggest it is possible to reflect on a particular place in terms of what can be called its "spiritual geography." Admittedly, this is different from the traditional theological task of examining and reconstructing belief. It is even beyond the exploration of the ways belief affects behavior, although it connects to that. It extends the theological enterprise into exploring how context influences faith. "Context" is a word often used to describe a particular environment, including its less physical dimensions, such as sociological, historical, cultural, and economic factors. Not only does context affect belief, it can also provide a grid or window through which one understands subsequent reality and, ultimately, how one relates to God.

Expanding the theological task to discern a particular locale's "spiritual geography" takes yet another factor into account. I consider "spiritual geography" the intermixing of attitudes, context, and environment, and the ways this clustering calls to the spirit, or squelches it. Although difficult to pinpoint, this new way to look at "place" teaches us much about what nurtures and what kills the spirit of a person. While each individual does bring a unique temperament, background, and volition to any environment, there are factors that affect attitude in somewhat predictable ways, and these can have significant spiritual outcome. Thus, I am suggesting that it is not just "holy" places (for example, places that inspire pilgrimage or shrines) that have a spiritual dimension—although many folk religions have long noted this—but all places.

Still, discerning a locale's "spiritual geography" could be reduced to a vague delineation of how the place is or is not conducive to human flourishing on the material level. To minimize this declension, I believe that two presuppositions undergird any theological exploration of "spiritual geography." These are, one, that God is continually trying to reach us, break through our defenses, permeate us with divine grace. And, two, as John Calvin stressed, that God accommodates to our condition. In other words, our particularity creates the need for God to come to us in ways we can understand, and fortunately for us, God has the consummate ability to do this.

Discerning an environment's "spiritual geography" is an enigmatic task. Therefore, it helps to focus on a locale one knows personally and feels viscerally. Although this is not always possible, it is advisable to become as intimate as possible with the place one wishes to describe. The common danger that I see in this task is choosing a place very dissimilar from one's own environment and then romanticizing, stereotyping, or deprecating it. Probably the most demanding requirement in all of this is an honest listening to and absorbing of the place, rather than simply importing one's particular agenda, however laudable it may be. Once this is functioning, religious reflection can emerge intuitively for persons with a faith stance and the habit of thinking theologically. One's particular faith commitments will, inevitably, affect the categories that emerge, but this need not relegate individual description to the purely subjective. Instead, it demonstrates the conjunction of environment and human perspective.

For the particular context of Newark—especially the North Ward, which I have examined microcosmically—I find that theological reflection clusters around three distinct sets of themes: first, sin, shame, and scapegoating; second, grace and beauty; and third, church and community. In all three of these, one's sense of and relationship to "place" factors in significantly.

Sin, Shame, and Scapegoating

For Newark, the images of being trapped in or pushed out, of defending, deserting, or moving on seem apt. These all display effort and exigency, rather than desire and ease. The urban environment thus is not placid or static. While some of the long history of residents moving away from Newark is due to its small size and its openness to newcomers, efforts to deal with the resultant crowding have sometimes had unintended consequences. Even if one brackets corruption and intentional mismanagement, it is evident that bad decisions—including those with beneficent intentions—can cause painful disruption, such as the overbuilding of public housing, inhospitable designs, or misguided attempts at urban renewal.

Yet there are more emotional and spiritual factors involved. From a theological perspective, we can discuss sin, shame, and scapegoating. "Bad press" and stereotyping such as Newark has suffered, may evoke as much shame and abandonment as the conditions that led to this labeling. For example, the evaluation—and even ranking—of locales is a common American dynamic. Periodicals regularly feature "Best of" lists commenting on quality of life, retirement, cost of living, employment opportunities, and so on. In the popular mind, Newark has not fared well in this contest. Yet this dynamic, which is common to many urban locales, not only reflects but can exacerbate desertion by the upwardly mobile or fearful.

It is difficult to know precisely how much of the mobility is valid self-determination and how much is abandonment that could be termed sinful. I only know that where once my extended family contained seventeen members who lived in Newark, today there are none. Most moved to nearby towns or to the Jersey shore. This very common pattern has been repeated by hundreds of thousands from Newark. Continuing their pattern of seeking the best education they could afford, my parents sent me to public high school in a nearby town and a college out of state. In both cases, my classmates expressed fear or repugnance about coming to Newark to visit. I felt there must be something implicitly wrong with my roots.

Yet moving up and out is the American way. We are a very transient society and, as a nation of immigrants, we habitually seek the greener grass and turn our backs on the past. This has contributed to our national vigor, yet it is not a purely innocent venture. Abandonment can leave desolation in its wake. Further, to look back with shame is self-destructive. To look back with nostalgia can prompt despair. To look back and laugh is even worse.

Equally important but less examined, however, is the effect on those left behind. There can be a blaming of the place and the people such that remaining residents feel not only abandoned, but trapped, unfortunate, victimized. The scapegoating of the poor can also play a part in less-than-optimal plans to deal with urban problems—such as the razing of Newark's First Ward and the ill-fated Columbus Homes. Scapegoating can be a way to deal with internal tensions within a community; it can reflect the "horizontal violence" of one disadvantaged group against another, as in the Newark riots and Kawaida Towers events.

According to Christian theology, no one is without sin. But we have not paid enough attention to the sinned-against and what that does to the spirit. Shame and a desire to emulate the deserters has a corrosive effect on the human spirit. It sets up a trajectory of escape that works against faith and a steadfast investment in one's current locale. Christian theology, however, also speaks to the surprising reality that God often comes to those of little prominence in unexpected ways and places. The fact that the divine incarnation came in the vulnerable form of a baby, resident in a small and insignificant place, to undistinguished parents, victimized by a larger system, holds a message of hope.

Grace and Beauty

Newark's North Ward is fortunate in having some impressive landmarks that give it a positive sense of place. Having beauty in one's midst—especially when it is accessible to the public—does help alleviate or control the feeling of being trapped and the desire to flee. These "placeholders," however, require tending. The Clark mansion, the Cathedral Basilica and Branch Brook Park all require commitment to remain viable and available. Some residents of the North Ward have rallied around these places, evoking personal investment from them and prompting it in others. These efforts of preservation and beautification help give grace a home.

When there is beauty for the senses, it calms the spirit. There seems less need to rush off or leave when one is already moved emotionally into a more peaceful and pleasing domain. That "state of grace" is a reminder that other dimensions exist beyond what is in our immediate sphere. The cathedral, with its visual and aural beauty and frank reference to divinity, was an obvious place for this. That it required some patience to receive the benefit only enhanced its effect.

But grace and beauty can also come in unexpected ways. On some days, feeling trapped can change into feeling safe and protected. Having to "stay put" coaxes one into opening up to surprises, if only because they are so needed. When attentive, we might notice how God's grace flows into these cracks in our perspective. Old brick looks especially handsome in afternoon light, even if the building itself has seen better days. A resident's grapevine with no space to grow except on a frame over the driveway looks plucky and charming. If all you can see is the top of a single tree from your apartment window, it is poignantly beautiful silhouetted against the sky. Grace coming this way can give a message of God's interest and presence.

People, too, can be carriers of grace. The shopkeeper who treats neighborhood children with respect, and the neighbor who patiently teaches a teenager to sew, are real-life examples. These ministrations can leave the lasting impression that we are worth attention and care. In fact, even a benign neglect can be beneficial if the resultant freedom allows traces of grace and beauty to break through. Thus, sometimes an inauspicious environment, by calling less attention to itself and requiring more effort from the observer, allows unexpected grace to get through our resistances.

Church and Community

Many people love city life. They often gain energy by the jostling and stimulation that comes from a diverse population and its products. However, as modern life has become more transient and bureaucratized, many people also feel anonymous, lost in the crowd, just a number for others to categorize or control. Humans, knowing implicitly that they are small and finite, can perceive themselves further dwarfed by the city's scale and size. Instead, we need our presence acknowledged and, better, appreciated. A manageably small neighborhood like the North Ward is one way to humanize city life. Being known "on the block" and in the shops, taverns, and restaurants roots a person and acknowledges legitimate human interdependency. In a community a person is part of a larger entity, not so alone, and this provides the spirit with soil in which to grow.

Just being part of a community is not in itself a guarantee of fertile soil for the spirit, however. Much depends on the personality and viability of the community. It is also necessary to have a more transcendent focal point. The church can provide this and also be another place urban people have a face. The glorious architecture of Sacred Heart, and many urban churches built during the heyday of American religion, witness to a larger goal than the day-to-day quest for survival and comfort. When one is part of a community of faith, oriented to God, meaning can be invested in the mundane.

Yet one can be relatively anonymous in the church, too. In my own experience, I found that the church did give me a wider vision, a sense of place, opened my eyes to beauty, and turned me toward God. However, it did not provide a tangible community where I was known. As I sat in the pew each Sunday—often by myself because of my family situation—I noted that many people came with relatives and seemed to know others there. For me, although I might occasionally glimpse people I recognized, there was little way I as a child alone could become engaged in the life of the congregation. Although attending the service was peaceful and contemplative, it was also lonely. In my extended observation, the functioning of the faith community clearly worked better for those who were accompanied, attended the parochial school, were of the same ethnic group as the clergy, and/or were able to contribute funds or time in a recognizable way. This obviously cuts out many of the people who need human recognition—as a reminder of God's care—in order for their spirits to flourish.

For many area residents, however, church and community were integrated into the whole of life. The same people could be seen at church, shopping, walking, working, and around the table. I noted that churchgoers stopped by our bakery on their way home in preparation for the big Sunday family dinner. In fact, our shop participated in the liturgical year by having particular confections distinctive to the various holidays and saints' days. All this is unlike the contemporary suburban pattern where often one's church community is entirely different from those people seen at work, in the mall, or near home. I believe it helps sustain realistic expectations for oneself and others, as well as enhances one's sense of place, to see fellow believers in many contexts, not just when they are "being religious."

Perhaps some would say I should never have left Newark; I should have stayed and helped the area. Yet the larger exodus seemed inexorably to sweep myself and my relatives along. My faith journey took me even farther away, into another state, another denomination, and to work entirely different from what anyone could have predicted. Had I not left for educational, employment, and spiritual opportunities, however, I doubt I would be writing this article today, be an ordained Presbyterian, or be teaching theology. It is true that the exodus theme is a legitimate one within the Christian ethos, and even Jesus had to leave Nazareth in order to be heard. But for those of us both nurtured by and propelled out of a place like Newark, the whole experience is bittersweet. This article itself, however, is a form of reconciliation. For while my spiritual trajectory took me far away from home, only in so doing have I gained the ability to verbalize and appreciate what I gained there—and realize who I was following when I left.

4
Degenerative Utopia in Philadelphia
Toward a Theology of Urban Transcendence
Mark Lewis Taylor

Pilgrims

It is early morning at Philadelphia's Sixth and Market streets, and already shiny tourist coaches are disgorging their passengers. They mill about, awaiting instructions from tour guides for their visit to the Liberty Bell and Independence Square, ready for making pilgrimage to the icons of the nation's civil religion, where the drafting of the U.S. Declaration of Independence and the Constitution are commemorated.

While representing many states, the tourists also form a multiethnic and multinational group. This is all the more evident when, by noon, tourists accumulate in greater numbers, from still more buses and cars. They are full of expectation. It is the July Fourth weekend, and even though the temperatures will reach close to 100 degrees this day, downtown Philadelphia is ready, as in many previous years, to offer itself for exhibition to these tourists who have come as so many pilgrims to a nation's sacred sites.

From the earliest days of the nation, Philadelphia has been a center for processions and exhibitions that seek to rehearse citizens in the nation's basic meanings and myths. In 1788 Philadelphia held a "Grand Procession" to celebrate ratification of the Constitution.[1] The procession's inclusion of many craftsmen and artisans anticipated what Philadelphia came to be, a city of manufacturing. The early commemorative and Federalist poet Francis Hopkinson referred to the city's manufacturing of many crafts, and to the founding fathers as craftsmen raising a "government firm" for the sake of a far-flung union. Hopkinson's poem about the new Constitution was entitled "The Raising: A Song for Federal Mechanics." Even as the new nation was raised in Philadelphia, the city itself was raised, organizing itself and its leaders by organizing the labor of its artisan classes. It harnessed that labor for growth in the Delaware Valley, becoming a first gateway to the West, developing a fur trade with indigenous peoples to the west and a maritime trade with nations to the east.

The pilgrim tourists of the twenty-first-century procession come from these and other distant regions, receiving their passes into Independence Square and hearing speeches from park rangers about the early colonists to the north who protested British taxation and eventually fought the battles of Lexington and Concord. The park ranger easily coaxes from schoolchildren some of the more familiar lines. "Do you remember what the Americans said when the British king made them pay taxes?" asks one ranger. "No taxation without representation," says a girl in the front row.

After this introduction in an air-conditioned room, the tourists are ushered into Independence Hall to see an early common law courtroom, then the assembly hall where the Constitution was debated and drafted. They tour the nearby Congress Hall where the first U.S. Senate and House meetings were held and where George Washington was inaugurated. Tourists are then encouraged to enjoy the rest of the day, visiting such sites as the Liberty Bell, the Tomb of the Unknown Soldier of the American Revolution, assorted churches from the colonial era, the First Bank of the United States, and more.

As these twenty-first-century pilgrims spill out into the city of today, finding shops, hotels, museums, and banks, they reenter a major metropolis that has developed remarkably since its founding. Though it soon lost its status as capital of the United States, and soon was replaced by New York City as the second-largest city in the world after London, it nevertheless cut its own distinctive profile as

> the commercial hub of a geographically central agricultural state. The development of banking and finance in the city was a response to this geography, as well as to the expansion and concentration of capital in the Delaware Valley during the Seven Years War (1754–63) and the American and French Revolutions. It was in these years that Philadelphia's merchants and financial leaders created the financial institutions that would be essential to industrial development in the nineteenth century: the Bank of North America (founded in 1781), the Bank of the United States (1791), the Philadelphia stock exchange (1792), the Bank of Pennsylvania (1794), and the various mutual fire and maritime insurance companies.[2]

After riding its diversified manufacturing economy to become a giant manufacturing center, by 1930 it was the third-largest U.S. city. Today Philadelphia, like many other urban areas, has transformed itself into a service-based, postindustrial city, using its July Fourth celebrations to craft its place in yet another union—not that of the United States but that of the global economic order. In fact, when former mayor Ed Rendell (now Pennsylvania's governor) set out to rescue the city from its waning manufacturing period, he did so by marketing the whole eight-county area of which Philadelphia is one part as a great "region" for global development.[3] At the center of that effort in political economy was the marketing of Philadelphia's Independence Square and the myths of making America there, the historic "miracle of Philadelphia." The tourists' pilgrimage today, then, is not just an exercise in political remembrance but also one of commercial significance. Yet this is hardly the whole story of Philadelphia.

Marchers

Ten blocks from where the pilgrim tourists assemble, it is also early morning at Philadelphia's Sixteenth and Market streets. There a very different group is coming together on the plaza just west of the City Hall building. It, too, will march to the Liberty Bell, albeit by a more circuitous route and with a different perspective. About five hundred tourists will wind their way through the streets, passing luxury hotels, a criminal justice building, the city's major newspaper offices, and crowded shopping districts. They will also stop at Thirteenth and Locust streets, where black journalist and activist Mumia Abu-Jamal was arrested in 1981 at the murder site of police officer Daniel Faulkner. Abu-Jamal was later convicted of the crime and has been on Pennsylvania's death row for over twenty years.

These marchers are fewer in number than the tourists, but they, too, are multiethnic and multinational. They have come by van, car, and subway, from Philadelphia neighborhoods lying to the north, south, and west of downtown. Some have driven from various college campuses across the country. Others have come from abroad.

These marchers move in observance of events very different from those commemorated by the pilgrims at the Liberty Bell. These marchers recall the arrest and imprisonment of Abu-Jamal, viewing them as a frame-up and travesty of justice.[4] They remember years of police brutality and corruption in 1970s and 1980s Philadelphia, the legacy of which they believe to be still alive now, after the turn of the century. They recall the city's use of a military explosive dropped from the air on the home of the MOVE Organization, which destroyed some sixty homes in a residential neighborhood, killing eleven people inside, five of them children.[5] They recall the decades of many initiatives by black leaders in the city, most of which were repressed, often brutally, by politicians and police raids. These marchers have no tour guides, but they have their inspiring and strong speakers, such as Pam Africa of the International Concerned Family and Friends of Mumia Abu-Jamal.

Listen to the marchers' speeches carefully, and you hear the construction of a history quite different from that relayed to the pilgrim tourists. It is a less glorious history, one that remembers that William Penn's Philadelphia was a gift bestowed upon him unilaterally by his family while he was still in England, and without regard to the habitation of indigenous Lenni Lenape, Conestoga, or Munsee populations in the Delaware River Valley.[6] Penn is usually given high marks for a Quaker tradition of tolerance, but the 8,000 Lenni Lenape on hand when he arrived were already much devastated from disease and warfare, such that more benign measures could be deployed by Penn to pacify them. When he founded the city in 1682, Penn grieved little for their decimation and expected them to move to the north and west as Philadelphians moved into new areas for fur trade and expansion.[7]

Listen to those marchers' speeches and you will hear the legacy of centuries of a Philadelphia that was built around the major concerns of an elite class. The crucial period was in 1830 to 1860, when Philadelphia's urban politics was built around the needs and wishes of a private elite. In his well-known book *The Private City,* Samuel Bass Warner says this period was crucial for establishing the city as belonging primarily to "private money makers."[8] During this period, the city's early artisan and journeyman classes were regimented into a major labor force, with longer hours, faster-paced production routines, increased social isolation, and economic insecurity.[9] Communitarian traditions generally, and especially among workers, were broken down.[10]

Corruption grew throughout the manufacturing era.[11] A political machine kept the Philadelphia elite atop the private city. "Philadelphia manufacturers tolerated the city's Republican machine because it produced a congressional delegation that consistently supported protective tariffs, shielding American industry from foreign competitors."[12] Warner's concluding paragraph in *The Private City* is telling:

> From first to last, the structure of Philadelphia had been such that, with the exception of the brief and creative union of equalitarian goals and business leadership in the early nineteenth century, no powerful group had been created in the city which understood the city as a whole and which wanted to deal with it as a public environment of a democratic society. In 1930, Philadelphia, like all large American cities, stood as a monument to the tradition of the private city.[13]

Listen to the marchers' speeches today, and you will hear them tell also of a long history of racism and poverty mutually compounding one another. By the 1970s, when manufacturing jobs started leaving the city and its postindustrial era was being born, large numbers of city neighborhoods had simply become disconnected from any structures of opportunity pertaining to jobs, housing, and quality of life.[14] Poverty resulted. "One recent study of the increase in pockets of urban deprivation in the 1970s reports that among America's fifty largest cities, Philadelphia fared the worst."[15]

Given that "the private city's" gentlemanly elite had always been primarily white, and given the "white flight" from troubled urban areas, the new impoverishment of Philadelphia took a heavier toll on neglected black communities. In 1960, 96.2 percent of blacks lived in impoverished areas.[16] In 1988, 23 percent of Philadelphia families below the poverty line were black, as opposed to only 4 percent of white families being below that line.[17] Even former Mayor Ed Rendell's "regionalist" program for situating Philadelphia in a global network did not redress the problem. The problem of poverty in fact increased. Census data in 1997, during Rendell's second term, showed that as much as a third of the entire city remained below the poverty line. Children's plight was worse, with anywhere between 29 and 52 percent of them in poverty.[18]

The entire city suffered as well. As it shrank from third-largest to fifth-largest in the United States, there was a 30 percent drop in the number of middle-income families. By 1990, 20 percent of the entire populace was at the poverty level; 35 percent were inadequately immunized against infectious disease; 40 percent of those enrolled in the urban education system dropped out in high school.[19] There are almost no sources that contest this record of decline—a loss for the entire community but a decline that especially reverberated through households and communities of the racially stigmatized poor of urban Philadelphia. Mistrust of Philadelphia elites' globalizing designs for the city is widespread among its poor, and is, in fact, well-founded, especially if we note some of the elites' own words. Rosemary Greco, CEO of CoreStates Bank and later head of the regional developers in "Greater Philadelphia First," exemplified the attitude:

> Regionalism is not about inner-city guilt, or helping the poor. It's
> about being able to compete in the world. It's not about correct-
> ing the past, but rather optimizing for the future. We need to
> develop this idea of globalization for people to understand
> regionalism.[20]

Understandably, then, some of these marchers will move
through the city with a sense that America has been betrayed, especially in Philadelphia. Others will level a more severe critique, that
"America" never was constructed in a way designed to function for
the full freedom of all. In whatever ways they spin the critique, the
marchers together offer a visual exhibit, contesting the celebration
at the city's pilgrimage site that only glosses the ugly reality of the
city's past and present.

As a group, the marchers will experience Philadelphia's security
forces very differently than will the tourists making pilgrimage to
the shrines. The pilgrims will be greeted by official park rangers
and then be escorted by them into Independence Park where the
Liberty Bell and other sites are found. This will involve standing in
line to pass through a security checkpoint, much as one would in
today's U.S. airports. Bags are screened, bodies stretched and
checked. Pilgrims emerge from the security building into a well-
guarded Independence Park. A glance around will show the site to
be well guarded. While the area was once open to passenger traffic,
it is now closed off. Waist-high concrete barriers and police fences
secure old access points. Armed guards are stationed at most of
these barrier areas. The pilgrims are well oriented and protected by
uniformed park rangers. In short, while the pilgrims are monitored
and controlled by security forces, they are actors undertaking
respected and authorized activity.

The marchers have a very different experience. Simply to gather
on site and conduct their march, they will have had to secure a special permit from the city, or, as marchers in Philadelphia have often
done, simply run the march without a permit—technically illegal,
but tolerated. Police officials gather in small pools around the rally
plaza, some in plain clothes, others in uniform, while marchers
make their preliminary speeches. Around the corner, police vans
with uniformed officers are ready on call in case the marchers get

out of hand and arrests have to be made. Police officers—again both in plain clothes and in uniform—will walk both ahead and behind the marchers, sometimes alongside on sidewalks. If police cannot contain marchers on sidewalks, which they usually cannot, they often try to limit them to one lane of the street, urging them also not to block intersections.

Relations between marchers and police range from cordial to strained to confrontational at times. After all, whatever the demeanor of an individual officer, it is the police who have guarded and often implemented the very designs of city politicians that marchers are protesting. Police have attacked marching crowds from behind with almost no provocation save abrasive rally chants. Marchers have surprised police before with unexpected actions, as when on July 3, 1999, nearly one hundred marchers put in motion a predesigned plan to close down the Liberty Bell building, ringing bells all around its perimeter, chanting "Let freedom ring for Mumia." Pilgrims were not able to resume visiting the Liberty Bell until hours later when police arrested the marchers.

Listen to the marchers' speeches again, and once more we learn that there has been a long history of law enforcement targeting the racially stigmatized poor and their activists in Philadelphia. Amid the abandonment of poor communities of color in the 1970s, the city, rather than meet the new economic and political needs for enfranchising the poor, chose to invest and use greater disciplinary and security measures. The racially stigmatized poor did not suffer this disenfranchisement passively. They organized creative and effective modes of resistance. This, however, only intensified the brutality of the city's forces, with police once actually entering a high school and clubbing youthful protestors working on programs organized by the Black Panthers and others.[21] This was especially true during the administrations of Frank Rizzo (the police chief who became city mayor).[22] The city soon saw police brutality and corruption rise to the point where an unprecedented lawsuit by the U.S. Department of Justice was lodged against the city.[23]

Philadelphia, in sum, can be interpreted as a collection of con-temporary visual exhibitions, whether they are the pilgrim tourists or the marching protestors. It is in Philadelphia's history of processions, exhibitions, and structures of control—and in the meanings of all of those—that we will find the milieu for a theology of the city.

Theology and the City

Theological reflection, with respect to the phenomena represented by cities, makes a particular contribution: it brings into focus and analyzes particular experiences of transcendence that often pervade the utopias that humans elaborate for urban planning and living. Thus, a theological reflection on cities is a form of "utopics," a form of studying and creating utopias.[24] It is, however, a particular mode of utopics, one that gives special thematic attention to the transcending dimension of urban utopias.

Dreaming of and projecting ideals have long been associated with cities. We need think not only of Thomas More's *Utopia* (1516), but also of Homer's infusion of ideals into the city-state Phaecia in the *Odyssey,* or Plato's consideration of the ideals of good governance as related to the city and citizens.[25] Jewish and Christian traditions have taken cities as examples both of utopia (the prophets' "New Jerusalem"; Augustine's "City of God") and dystopia (Babylon; Sodom and Gomorrah). Critical geographer David Harvey notes that the city's rising and, especially, its falling, are inscribed in the great dystopias of Aldous Huxley's *Brave New World* or George Orwell's *1984.*[26]

The making of utopias has frequently been criticized, of course. Karl Marx has disparaged utopianism, but this was more a necessary critique of a devastating free-market utopianism than it was of all or any utopian reflexes in human desire. Marx had his own utopian impulses in the sense that he projected ideals for the future that he desired to see instantiated in real life.[27] Postmodernists have criticized the colonizing and regimenting desires of modernity's classic utopias, and contemporary feminists have joined them to advocate for various alternative "heterotopias" to counter the classic utopias of largely male desires.[28] Even these heterotopias, however, reflect not the absence of utopian reflection, but its reformulation.[29] It is in the idealizing and dreaming dimensions of urban utopias that a theology of cities will find the transcending qualities that are its special subject matter.

But what is meant by "transcending" or "transcendence"? These terms have a long and problematic history in the developments of theology and philosophy of religion. For some, these terms connote unverifiable and otherworldly experiences of religion that have no place in rational discourse, nor in the technological disciplines of urban planning and daily life. Transcendence is identified by its distance from natural and human life forms, its "otherness."

For others, and in this essay, the term "transcendence" suggests a more dialectical relation, a mutual entailment, between a distant, "other" quality and the natural quality of everyday human dynamics. Here, transcendence is marked not just by distance and otherness, but also by a special quality of relations that exist *within* this worldly human and cultural life. Indeed, this special quality will often hint at "something more" than the sum total of natural and human cultural life forms, be they particular myths, spiritual visions, religious beliefs, doctrines, or rites; nevertheless, this "something more" is always mediated in and through—never known apart from—those natural and human life forms.

City utopias seek to realize transcendence in many ways. One of the most frequent is noted by Graham Ward in his *Cities of God* (2000), in which he observes that cities often seek transcendence "in the sublime heights of their towers." Cities go beyond by going up, we might say, engineering "the euphoria of the sublime through panoramic vistas offered from these towers."[30] This kind of urban transcendence is an experience of the sublime that is more in keeping with the first notion of transcendence, dependent on distance from a lower spatial world.

Ward develops his own theological response to the city with more nuance, with a greater dialectical understanding of transcendence, one that focuses on the quality of relations in city life. He gives special prominence to developing his theology in response to two major challenges of urban life: first, that of preserving bodily desire and human connection to nature, and second, that of fostering human unity in the face of the "social atomism" and unjust divisions that city living often generates.[31]

Intriguingly, these two areas for seeking transcendence in urban life were also present in an early formulation by Paul Tillich in 1928. In that year, Tillich addressed the Dresden Technical Institute at the school's centennial celebration.[32] There he reflected on the ways humans, when constructing cities, often also project ideals that they seek to live out. Although global cities have become many things that were unknown in 1928 Dresden,[33] or in any city at Tillich's death in 1965, Tillich's ruminations on the structural challenges posed to building and maintaining large cities still wear well today.

The building and maintenance of cities, writes Tillich, are troubled by two major threats. First, there is an alienation from material nature. Amid the frenetic pace and dynamism of technologized nature in the city, which creates a certain delight and celebration of bodily desire, there persists, still, a certain lifelessness in the city that grows in the urbanized human. "The soil, the bond with the living earth, is taken away. Hewn or artificial stone separates us from it. Reinforced concrete buildings [he doesn't mention plastic and steel] separate us more than loam, wood and bricks from the cosmic flow."[34] Against this major threat, in Tillich's view, there must be a reconnecting to the vitality of nature, a move similar to Ward's efforts to reconstitute bodily desire.

Second, for Tillich, there is the threat of alienation from one another. Tillich explicitly has in mind here the alienation of workers who are mobilized to build the technical city and who become alienated from those who enjoy or use it. The city, then, for all its advantages, holds a major threat to the unity that human beings need one with another if they are to live well. This is not just a general alienation of humans from one another, nor is it just the problem of fragmentation and "social atomism" that is such a prominent concern in Ward's treatment of the city. It is a split suffered, particularly, by the city's builders: the men, women and, historically, children, all those "most deeply involved in the service of the technical city . . . who have nothing to make up for the powers of life of which they have been deprived, who do indeed have dominion over things, but nevertheless as ones who are themselves ruled over, stunted in their vital and spiritual life: the proletariat."[35]

These reflections by Tillich allow us to return to the notions of transcendence and utopia in urban living. Ideal transcending qualities in urban utopia and life will be those that resist the major threats posed by the loss of connectedness to nature and also by the alienation of atomized groups from one another. Put positively, such resistance also imagines a future and fuels work toward that future, in which urban desire and living are reoriented to the city's belonging to nature—and in which urban groups are restored to a mutual interaction characterized by social justice and peace between them. It is such relations that constitute the qualitative transcendence of urban utopia, upon which theologians of the city do well to reflect.

Urban utopias, which yield structures that fail to withstand the two major threats here discussed, can be termed, following Louis Marin, "degenerative utopias,"[36] those that yield greater loss of vital connection to nature or greater alienation of groups to one another. Degenerative utopias create and compound oppression. The aim of a theologian of the city is to counter degenerative utopias with preferred, regenerate ones. This will involve the identification and embodiment of alternative, symbolic practices for restoring and maintaining urban citizens' desires in relation to nature and for restoring and maintaining justice and peace in the city. A theology that reflects upon and supports resistance and dreaming toward such utopias, in the face of oppressive effects of degenerative utopias, belongs to the theologies of liberation. The theology of the city, in this sense, envisions and works toward a theology of integral liberation.

It must be acknowledged that this understanding of liberation for the city is not based only on a theologians' study of ambiguities and threats attending cities. It is also rooted in theologians' own particular interpretations of their traditions, from which they derive certain notions of transcendence. It must remain beyond the scope of this essay, however, to discuss the features of Christian faith that have encouraged my focus here on the two foci of urban transcendence that are crucial for regenerative utopias in the city.[37]

A full theology of the city, be it for Philadelphia or for other cities, would entail imaginatively constructing many symbolic and doctrinal elements in a regenerative utopia for cities. I do not undertake that here, because it is a crucial precondition for elaborating a regenerative utopia that we first understand *de*generative utopia. In the next section, therefore, I present a portrait of the structure of degenerate utopia.

The American Manufactory in Philadelphia: A Degenerative Utopia

Philadelphia from its beginnings has had a strong utopian aspiration. Its very name, "city of brotherly love," bespeaks that aspiration. It was to be a good place, indeed, a kind of asylum for persecuted members of the Society of Friends, the Quakers, and "for the oppressed of all nations."[38] In fact, Philadelphia has been more a negative utopia, with its ideals structured in ways that set degenerative trends in motion from the outset.

We are helped in examining these trends by turning to Laura Rigal's splendid analyses in her book *The American Manufactory: Art, Labor and the World of Things in the Early Republic* (1998). Her notion of the "manufactory" is crucial for discerning the degenerative structure of the city's systems and practices.

What is a manufactory? It is different from the concrete, industrial processes of manufacturing that we can observe in factory and workplace, although as a process of production it is related to what goes on in those sites. A manufactory is an "array of visual and legible representational technologies," or "visual frameworks of exhibition" that lie behind, are carried within, manufacturing systems, and which are often replicated in other realms of the cultural order. These are representational practices that register the way a city relates to its natural environment, positions human bodies one to another, disperses work energies and organizes new labor pools, arranges social interaction, and disseminates meanings, ideals, and visions throughout the system. The manufactory is a process of structuring what sociologist Pierre Bourdieu termed a people's *habitus*, their acquired habits and tactics for using and being in the body and in the world.[39]

A manufactory is continually emerging, though often hidden, within many cultural realms. It is a framing and working activity. It goes on within cultures using the machinery and the relations operative in manufacturing production. In Philadelphia and the Delaware Valley, Rigal refers to the manufactory as "the uneven, multiform, and variously mediated *quality of industrialization* in early national Philadelphia, where partial or experimental mechanization frequently accompanied the rationalization of labor and where such changes assumed a remarkable variety of forms across more than fifty crafts or 'trades.'"[40]

This structural "quality of industrialization," the manufactory, operates by means of three dynamics: division, erasure, and creating of spectators. Each of these dynamics builds upon the preceding one. This manufactory did not only work in Philadelphia, hence Rigal refers to it, more nationally, as "the *American* manufactory." Nevertheless, it had its first most striking embodiment in early Philadelphia, and the city, as well as the nation founded there, wrestle with the legacy of that manufactory and its dynamics.

The first dynamic is *division,* a class division, and it can be seen at work during the very time of the city's celebration of the Constitution's ratification. I have already alluded to this period, in which ratifying the Constitution for the new union was seen as analogous to raising a roof on a dwelling place. At the same time, both kinds of "raising" were also seen as analogous to the work of Federalist planners of the Constitution, such that they themselves could be depicted as the craftsmen or mechanics of a complex building's operations. The effect was to portray the act of raising the Constitutional roof over the republic as an act not only done by workers (even though the Federalist planners certainly were not) but also as good for the workers.

One might actually think that in a celebration that portrays founding fathers as mechanics that we would find an egalitarian respect and positive regard for the worker. To the contrary, as Rigal shows in a close reading of Hopkinson's commemorative poem, pools of workers are depicted as lads and laborers who use their bodies and tools to assure the position of representatives above them in the new government. They hand up girders to build a roof that they as workers stand under. They also hand over a dignity, their own, giving it up to the congressmen: the white landowners and writers of the constitutional document who are the "sons of Columbia" standing in the center of government, "o'er the whole to preside."[41] Hopkinson also lampooned anti-Federalist measures that sought to give workers a more direct voice in government in another of his Federalist poems, "The New Roof." It ridicules the earlier Articles of Confederation (1781–1789) in ways that reveal class division and indeed legitimize that division. "Because of the failures of this old 'flat' roof [the Articles], the new roof must be 'raised'—but not only in the sense of simply being put into place (designed, ratified, and instituted). It must also be elevated—or raised at its center, pyramid-style—in order to keep its 'servants' down, in their place, and presumably, at work."[42]

Thus, there is discernible here the emergence of a class distinction, a transformation of artisans into workers who are under a roof maintained by a Federalist elite, having power that is not only political (as rulers, and with white and male entitlements) but also economic. "By identifying the 'authors' of the Constitution with the social rank of the skilled craftsmen (to which, again, virtually no leading Federalist belonged), [Hopkinson's song] displays the founding structure of American constitutionalism as class division, and class division as that line at which words themselves become objects when construction frames the state."[43]

This legacy of a class division has persisted throughout the long history of Philadelphia, much discussed by scholars as a private city failing to generate a communitarian ethos or agenda.[44] This Federalist elitism lives on today in the way corporate elites, together with Philadelphia mayors and other politicians, fuse their celebration of the nation's origins for attracting tourists with their marketing agenda for making patriotic pilgrimage the center of their city's new "regionalist" strategy. Mayor Rendell's own biographer, who generally was favorably disposed to the mayor, himself observed the class division that results when celebrating patriotism and entertainment supplants giving real assistance and empowerment to the city's urban poor.

> The trend of tourism raised the specter of a city workplace increasingly made up of waiters, ushers, tour guides, busboys, bellboys, sales clerks and interactive cyber helpers, an image that seemed bitterly ironic given the city's historic place as the best embodiment of American work. . . . Like his brethren across the country, he [Rendell] was working to rebuild and reinvent a wholly new place. . . . City as place to frolic for a few days on a convention, City as Six Flags for suburbanites looking for a weekend break from the monotony. . . . City increasingly fashioned and designed not for those who lived within it but for those who never would.[45]

Crucial to the American manufactory, then, and a structural condition of Philadelphia's degenerate utopia, is its continual maintenance of class division.

Erasure is a second dynamic of the American manufactory. I have already hinted at this dynamic, since the class division mentioned above also involved a certain erasure—an erasure of artisan workers' collectives. The division between Federalist author and artisan craftsman was glossed by referring to the authors of the Constitution as "mechanics." The real power and creativity of artisans—which commanded enormous respect and power throughout the colonial era in the colonies, especially as creative journeyman collectives—are obscured. Before the Federalist subordination of artisans into a labor pool, workers had considerable power to control their wage and work conditions.[46] As class division occurs, so these artisan collectives undergo erasure.

Erased along with artisans, of course, were the working lives of women. Throughout the Federalist period, women worked as "cooks, washerwomen, laundresses, private nurses, and renters of houses."[47] There were often "Ladies Branches" within the journeyman collectives, within which women's skillful organizing often defied their "branch" status, being able to shake the whole "tree."[48] Women had long been, in Philadelphia and throughout the colonies, effective organizers of riots against British *and* American officials, in resistance to corrupt shopkeepers and land owners. They conducted nearly one-third of the food riots in late eighteenth-century America.[49] A "motley crew" of multiracial workers rioted in this period, with women often playing leading roles, thus creating the social space that enabled the Federalists to form their union.[50] Later, however, Federalist framers hardly honored the work of those resisters, male or female. They had to be repressed, erased, and rendered invisible. When they did pay limited homage to a "noble worker," it was usually to a male.[51]

There are two other erasures, however, that intersect the erasures by class and gender. In the Philadelphia Grand Procession of 1788, Benjamin Rush waxed eloquent about the role of cotton textile production, which, "cultivated in the South and manufactured in the eastern and middle states," would enable "a bond of union . . . more powerful than any article of the New Constitution."[52] Here is a dramatic case of Federalism's continual erasure of the forced labor of African slaves, of which Rush here made no mention. Rigal argues that enslaved labor was "the face of union most deeply buried, or most emphatically excluded, by the exhibitionary Edifice of 1788."[53]

Few scholars of Philadelphia have looked deeply into Philadelphia's connections to the slave trade. William Penn and the Quakers were invested in the trade and imported slaves.[54] Some Quakers had come to Philadelphia from the West Indies where they established their wealth through slave labor. Samuel Powell Jr. was one of the "weightiest of Quakers" and was a slave merchant,[55] a fact omitted by sociologist E. Digby Baltzell when discussing Powell in his study *The Philadelphia Gentlemen.*[56]

Some 10,000 to 20,000 African slaves were brought to Philadelphia before the American Revolution.[57] Many Africans came straight from the West Coast of Africa to be sold off the ships into Philadelphia. In the colonies as a whole, at the time of ratification, about one-fifth of residents were black, although the ratio in Philadelphia was sometimes larger and sometimes smaller in comparison to that of other cities.[58]

Allen Ballard suggests that it was the longstanding connection of Philadelphia elites to slave-holding elites in the South (through economic dependence and intermarriage) that drove Philadelphia authorities to keep local urban black populations in a virtual state of "terror" by police brutality and by tolerating white race riots in black communities.[59] Even the much-celebrated "freed" blacks of Philadelphia felt the force of white fear working upon them. This was evident, for one example, in the wake of the 1831 Nat Turner Uprising in Virginia. Soon afterward, legislators in Pennsylvania and Philadelphia strengthened slave laws against blacks, even proposing legislation to curtail rights of "the freedmen" in Philadelphia.[60] The legacy of erasing black enslavement, and the practice of repressing black resistance, is alive in the twenty-first century's continuing neglect of African American urban Philadelphians and the repression of their activists.

The other important erasure that needs to be highlighted is that of indigenous peoples in the Delaware Valley. It is not surprising that Indians were erased from Constitutional celebrations. They had long been seen as destined for absence. As historian Thomas Merrell shows, the colonizers drew a sharp distinction between "the woods" and their own "inhabited part of the country." The woods were "the *un*inhabited," yet also the place where the Indians lived. Indians, then, were present/absent ones. As linked to the "uninhabited" woods, their presence was at best temporary, soon to end.

Just how widely disseminated was this dynamic of Indian erasure is evident in another cultural realm of the Philadelphia-based American manufactory—in the visual exhibitions of Philadelphia ornithologist Alexander Wilson. He collected over five-hundred bird specimens, and his nine-volume *American Ornithology* was published in Philadelphia between 1807 and 1814. Rigal depicts him as exemplifying the values that Thomas Jefferson delineated in his *Notes on the State of Virginia,* in which the ideal citizen of the union is a kind of agrarian husbandman who unites explorer and settler: "federal mechanic and family man."[61]

In his study of American birds, Wilson uses bird behavior and migration as an extended metaphor for the colonial federation of the North American land mass. Many of his textual descriptions of various bird behaviors are seen as emblems of ideal Federalist citizenship (especially the behavior of the "noble" Kingbird).[62] Wilson's bird books take to "logical republican extension" the metonym of "the nest," which Thomas Jefferson had also used for referring to the young United States, from which "all America, north and south, is to be peopled."[63] Rigal thus refers to a "feathered federalism" in which the new union is understood as "a phenomenon of produc-

tion and its migratory reproduction."[64] Wilson's collecting of specimens and the creation of a voluminous bird catalog represented the
domestication of the land and, we might add, aestheticized the settlers' colonizing migration by resorting to the colorful speciation of
birds and their imagined "colorful" behaviors and personalities.

Indian erasure, while "the nest" expands, is also registered in
Wilson's somewhat bizarre encounter with an ivory-billed woodpecker. The bird is a striking American species, reaching twenty
inches in height, crowned with a red topknot, featuring a long ivory
bill. Wilson analogizes this bird to the Indians whom, he claims,
will never be adopted or assimilated. They, like this woodpecker,
are doomed to extinction. This bird (today, indeed, nearly extinct)
is a "royal hunter . . . the king or chief of his tribe . . . ornamented
with carmine crest and polished ivory." Its ornamentation is like
that of "the southern tribes" (that is, the Creek, Seminole, Choctaw,
and Chickasaw) who, he notes, use bird feathers in their ornamentation customs.

When traveling in regions of "the southern tribes," Wilson actually captured an ivory-billed woodpecker in the woods of North
Carolina. He kept it alive under cover as an image for sketches.
When he entered Wilmington, the bird screamed in captivity with
the "violent crying of a young child," so much so that people anx-
iously offered Wilson lodging for him and "his baby." When he
uncovered the "baby" for onlookers, they were relieved and gath-
ered round for laughter. Then, the woodpecker's fate:

> Left in Wilson's hotel room, the woodpecker wreaks havoc,
> breaking a fifteen-inch hole through the wall, covering the bed
> with plaster, and nearly escaping. Wilson tries tying the bird to a
> mahogany table—upon which it likewise "wreaked his whole
> vengeance," nearly destroying it. While taking drawings of him,
> Wilson reports, the woodpecker "cut me severely in several
> places" and "displayed such a noble and unconquerable spirit
> that I was frequently tempted to restore him to his native woods.
> . . . He lived with me nearly three days, but refused all suste-
> nance, and I witnessed his death with regret."[65]

Visible in this account of the Philadelphia ornithologist's treatment
of this Indian-like bird are numerous points reflective of the Amer-

ican manufactory's mode of erasing Indians: romanticizing them (their unconquerable spirit), viewing them as associated with the undomesticated forest (native woods), caricaturing them as having a penchant for destructive violence, forcibly removing them from their places of habitation, and leaving them to a piously regretted death.[66] Note that with this particular erasure of the indigenous, the American manufactory also involves an opposition of the settler community to nature and a way of relating to it that is largely one of domination and control. Nature and its woods are to settlers as Indians and birds are to settlers, that is, destined for use, domination, and ordered control.

Intrinsic to the American manufactory at work at Philadelphia is a third dynamic, *the creation of respectful spectators*. Given the first two dynamics, of class division and erasure, and the tensions that they each engender, it is crucial that the American manufactory resort to spectacle. Spectacles excite, charm, mesmerize, and tend to enshrine and legitimate the present order. The Grand Processions at the time of the Constitution's ratification, which occurred in many East Coast colonial cities, were an example of this use of spectacle.[67] Wilson's ornithological display of the continent's aviary treasure, with all its colonizing meanings, is another. Class divisions and erasures tend not to be questioned when they are clothed with the power of spectacle.

The dynamic of creating respectful spectators in Philadelphia has relied on creating and sustaining two kinds of spectacle: spectacles of origin and spectacles of force.

We have already noted the city's spectacles of origin: the pilgrim tourists' celebrations at the nation's sacred sites. Philadelphia has fed these spectacles since the earliest days of the union. "The mechanics of a mass-mediated culture were a way of life in Philadelphia from its first days as a federal city. The arts of spectatorship, commemoration, collection, and display were structural to the political economy of nation-making at a place and time crisscrossed by economic, political, and cultural innovations that were restructuring the mechanical arts and constituting a domestic or 'home' economy in the United States."[68]

This long tradition has reached a new frenzy in the present, especially since recent Philadelphia administrations have made a concerted effort to market its spectacles of origin as a way to revive a faltering city economy. Sociologists such as Jerome Hodos have noted this recent emphasis.[69] Anthropologists, too, have observed the new accenting of this patriotic history-making, which largely is responsible for Philadelphia remaining "the fifth largest national television market and an important point on national film distribution."[70] Outside the United States, many identify the city almost immediately with "America."[71] Philadelphia continues to succeed in creating a national and global spectatorship, one that seeks continually to renew utopian dreams and economic recovery through its spectacles of origin.

There are, however, other kinds of spectacle that belong to this dynamic of the American manufactory: the spectacles of force. Displayed force is evident in the city. It is encountered in different ways by the pilgrim tourists, who line up to go through checkpoints and are led in orderly groups through sites by park rangers, and by the marchers, who are followed and monitored by police along their walks.

Philadelphia's longstanding tradition of building civic order upon institutions of force is evident in several engravings by an early nineteenth-century artist, William Russell Birch. Of special note is his *State-House Garden, Philadelphia* (1800), which was included in a book of his engravings that lay in the visiting room of Thomas Jefferson during the whole of his presidency.[72] This image features a near-idyllic setting of well-dressed women and men sitting and walking beneath trees and on park lawns. Beyond the wall of the park, viewable through the trees, accessible though the grand doorways of the park, is the Walnut Street Gaol (Jail). This juxtaposition of civilized garden and jail, again, gets at the heart of the life dreamed for Philadelphia and the nation. A hidden dimension of the American manufactory is disclosed:

> The juxtaposition of the (exit from the) garden with the (opaque windows of the) jail constitutes a reflection upon the visual architecture of social discipline: *confinement and control lies behind the*

open viewing space of the park-like garden. . . . . The prison windows behind the trees articulate a structure of solitude or isolation behind the mixed crowd, *connecting punishment with natural liberty*. . . . In places such as the "State House Garden," Birch's Views of 1800 brings the Grand Federal Edifice of 1788 into view once more as a commercial scaffolding raised into view over people who emerge within it *as viewing subjects and objects surveyed* . . . as a technographic phenomenon, the "New Roof" of 1788 not only represented but *enforced Union.*[73]

Rigal also discusses the romanticized portrait of a locksmith, *Pat Lyon at the Forge* (1829), by painter John Neagle. Lyon is shown in his forge as a well-dressed bourgeois laborer (shiny buckles, clean shirt, and all), with his artisan coworkers erased. Only he is featured in posed image. More tellingly, however, looming in an upper corner of the portrait is the Walnut Street Gaol, where Lyon had been confined before being exonerated of false charges for bank theft. The jail tower looms to haunt his restored and refurbished status.[74] It reminds viewers, just as Birch's engraving had, that civic life and pursuit of vocational freedom are marked by being non-jailed, by being positioned against the backdrop of jailed populations. The spectacle of force is intrinsic to public order. The degeneracy uncovered here is not the mere presence of the prison, or of force, but in the use of imprisoning force for the construction of identity, government, "civility," and enjoyment of nature.

Such a trait of the American manufactory would seem to be continuing into the twentieth and twenty-first centuries in the policies and practices of district attorneys (such as Ed Rendell and Lynn Abraham) and mayors (such as Rendell and Frank Rizzo) whose primary modes of urban control and structuring have relied on the use of force. This comes in the form of nearly unqualified support for law enforcement, in continuing problems of police brutality and corruption,[75] in big spending on prisons, and in commitments to make Philadelphia "the capital of capital punishment," as announced by district attorney Lynn Abraham, who served Rendell's administration and still serves the present one.[76] Mainstream viewers of "the miracle at Philadelphia" rarely glimpse one of the city's truths: that the federated union of citizens and civil society is rooted in coercion and force.

In sum, the American manufactory at work in Philadelphia is a quality of production, cultural and technological, evident in many cultural realms (work, gender relations, wildlife studies, westward expansion, and more). Three dynamics operate wherever the manufactory is at work: the dynamics of class division, of erasure (of artisans, women, slaves and African Americans, Indians, nature) and of creating respectful spectators (through spectacles of origin and spectacles of force).

These dynamics constitute the structure of degenerate utopia in Philadelphia. Whatever its utopian dreams and aspirations, the prevalence and enduring character of this American manufactory have kept the city steeped in forces of degeneration, historically and in the present. But what of its future? Can a theology of the city articulate a transcendence that fosters regenerative utopia, a set of aspirations, dreams, and practices that might prefigure and configure a better future for Philadelphia?

Toward Transcendence in the City

In the Bruce Springsteen video for his song "Streets of Philadelphia," the camera lens first zooms in from above City Hall, then, from even a higher vantage point, it closes in on the sparkling, pyramidal skyscrapers of downtown. It next sweeps across scenes of children playing around statues of founding fathers, of firemen readying shiny engines for duty, of suspension bridges leaping over the Delaware River into business centers, and, finally, of children filing by a very cracked Liberty Bell.

Then the video screen washes completely blue, filled only with wide-open sky. Slowly the camera view moves down through light cloud cover over Philadelphia, settling this time not upon any glittering skyscraper transcendence, but upon a trashed lot of weeds, scrubby bushes, and scattered stone. Deteriorating housing of poor urban America borders this lot. Nearby homeless men are shown warming themselves over a makeshift fire that blazes in a battered steel oil drum. Across this piece of urban blight the singer walks, unkempt and uncombed, muttering his song's opening lines, "I was bruised and battered and I couldn't tell what I felt."

Where is urban transcendence, any regenerate utopia, in such a landscape as this? When the utopian vistas of city founders, urban planners, and skyscraper architects are shown to be degenerate, as the ruthless structural powers of the American manufactory in Philadelphia so bleakly expose, then how dare we speak of transcendence in the city?

The trash-strewn urban field, showing blighted ground and foliage as well as the plight of homeless humanity upon it, depicts urban life crumbling under the threats of alienated nature and alienated human groups. In the American manufactory, these two threats have always been present, and now they challenge theologians' efforts to speak of transcendence in the city.

The Springsteen video could have used even more dramatic symbols of the city's degenerate state. It could have accessed public television archives to find footage of scenes of tree-lined streets in West Philadelphia consumed in fire and death—a near-apocalyptic symbol, if there ever was one, of an urban government unleashing destructive power against both its own natural environment and its own residents.[77] In this event's aftermath, novelist John Edgar Wideman caught the weight of that dramatic moment in 1985 and also its historic and political import.

> The whole city seen the flames, smelled the smoke, counted the body bags. Whole world knows children murdered here. But it's quiet as a grave, ain't it? Not a mumbling word. People gone back to making a living. Making some rich man richer.[78]

> These ruins. This Black Camelot and its cracked Liberty Bell burn, lit by the same match that ignited two blocks of Osage Avenue. Street named for an Indian tribe. Haunted by Indian ghosts—Schuylkill, Manayunk, Wissahickon, Susquehanna, Mayamensing, Wingohocking, Tioga—the rivers bronzed in memory of their copper, flame-colored bodies, the tinsel of their names gilding the ruined city.[79]

Amid the ruins of the city, any hope for a regenerate utopia, any encounter with transcendence, must intentionally, structurally, and consistently redress the city's broken connection to nature, and the broken and alienated relations between groups in the city. This latter task will especially have to redress the long-neglected needs and opportunities of the city's racially stigmatized poor—among them African American and indigenous peoples of the Delaware Valley. Only this kind of work embodies the concrete and qualitative mode of transcendence outlined above.[80]

Contemporary Philadelphia has long been abundant with communities—social services, community organizations, labor groups, grassroots movements, some churches and other religious organizations—which have sought to redress the city's alienation from nature and the alienation of many of its subordinated peoples. Those subordinated peoples have themselves generated resistance and communities that tackle the alienating threats, and hence model the kind of transcendence most needed. Many of these groups are still at work. There is the Kensington Welfare Rights Union, which for years now has foregrounded the rights of the poor and sought to redress the city's failure to provide for its most needy residents. The MOVE Organization remains, in spite of decades of police assaults and intimidation, a community of political struggle and spirituality, revering, as it says, the fundamental force of Life ("Mama Nature") as it continues its work on behalf of its imprisoned members. The International Concerned Family and Friends of Mumia Abu-Jamal, which organizes so many of the "marchers" noted earlier, remains an organization whose leaders routinely call for the city's renewed respect for nature and ecology, as well as for liberation and justice for Abu-Jamal and the host of persons imprisoned unjustly. The Simple Way, the School of the Americas, the Underground Seminary, the magazine *The Other Side*—these are all some of Philadelphia's many other groups that unite residents, within and without religious communities, in a struggle against all forms of structural alienation.

Here, however, we are less concerned with discussing the many particular communities that might undertake important work in the city and more with highlighting the new structural practices that any of these communities might manifest as transcending spirit at work in the city. Simply to dare to imagine new structural practices for implementation, perhaps, would begin to birth regenerative utopia in the city.

What are some of these new structural practices of transcending spirit, which might bring to life a more regenerate utopia in Philadelphia? As a response to this question, we cannot here give a blueprint or list of specific actions. Nor can we expect our utopian visions of regenerative urban life to be fully concretized. We can, however, point to *types of actions* that imaginatively address each of the three dynamics of degenerative utopia we have found to be at work in Philadelphia:[1] (1) class division and alienation, (2) erasure, and (3) the spectacles of the privileged and powerful. Consider each in turn.

Imagine a mobilized and imaginative resistance to class division and alienation in Philadelphia. Diverse communities—be they Christian, Muslim, Jewish, or other spiritual traditions and secular movements of conscience for justice and peace—might each make the divisive facts of poverty and racism their central concerns for being and action. Christian churches in particular have the unfortunate tendency of relegating the problems of poverty and racial injustice to the category of optional activities for, say, a "Church and Society Committee" in their institution, in which a few of its more principled members might participate. The bulk of such churches' activity then gets focused on other faith and religious matters that are purportedly more central to Christian faith.

In contrast to this tendency, actions redressing class division, racial inequality, and the division of peoples from nature need to be moved to the center of religious communities' worship life and regular practice. The necessary structural practices for urban justice need to be freed from their captivity in the church committees that only sometimes act successfully and only sometimes are supported by the whole religious community.

This could lead to far more dramatic and effective actions against the divisions of class, race, and humans from nature than we have seen heretofore. Imagine diverse communities of spirit opening their doors, regularly, for labor union meetings, and integrating the laments of the poor and of workers into their worship services or into their most important meetings. Imagine communities of spirit that motivate their members to meet workers in their neighborhoods, in the streets, and elsewhere, to plan actions for further liberating and healing activity. Imagine communities of spirit that enable city dwellers to dwell with and in a protected natural ecology, in which air remains clean, plants and trees thrive, and water flows to nourish all. In these ways urban communities resist both the alienation of humans from one another, and the alienation of human society from natural habitat.

To date, churches of nearly all ethnic backgrounds in Philadelphia have usually decided to make friends first with the powerful, with the elites whose regionalist agendas for the city's role in a globalization rarely serves the long-neglected urban poor or the needs of all communities to be in living connection with nature amid urban living. A truly transcending spirit would lead religious communities of the future to break their habits of currying favor with the powerful who routinely tend to sow more division and alienation.

Imagine a courageous celebration of the presence of groups that the powerful in Philadelphia's long history have so often tended to consign to erasure. Envision new communities that render present, in memory and new communal practice, not only poor male workers, but also women and women-led movements from all backgrounds, African and African-American communities of the city, as well as the indigenous peoples of the Philadelphia and Pennsylvania region whose legacy lingers, for example, in the many street names of the city (Osage, Schuylkill, Susquehanna, et al.). Throughout Latin America today and elsewhere, it is a frequent practice to draw present-day strength from those lost or unjustly slain in the past, by remembering them with a shouting affirmation, "¡Presente!" ("Let them be present!") In African-influenced communities the analogous affirmation is the West African "Ashe!" ("So be it!"). Such empowering remembrances are already at work in some communities of spirit in Philadelphia, often among the New Afrikan community, the International Concerned Family and Friends of Mumia Abu Jamal, and various church groups. Such remembrances do well to break forth with still greater frequency and power elsewhere.

When envisioning the end of these erasures, an important warning is in order, especially for those communities that have once been exclusive and now seek to "include" those long erased. Remembering and making present, after centuries of destructive erasure, means far more than simple inclusion and opening up a community's membership. It means reorienting the new communities of remembrance to the leadership, the resistance and the liberating strategies that those groups themselves have forged in their struggle against erasure. For the truth is that erased peoples have survived, often with their own dignity intact and their movements in place. Re-membering them means acknowledging this, their own enduring, re-constituting power and presence.

Imagine new communities—be they churches, other religious communities, or other peoples of conscience and spirit—that create their own new spectacles and their own artistic performances to celebrate visions of a regenerative utopia in Philadelphia. Spectacles are not "mere spectacles," just some "show" that organizers might do without. Rather, communities of regenerative utopia need more spectacles, spectacles of liberation and healing. This is especially true in a city like Philadelphia, which has from its beginnings used exhibitions and spectacles to consolidate the hold of white and commercially privileged classes over those racially stigmatized and many other poor groups. Philadelphia's "spectacles of origin," beginning with the Grand Procession that celebrated the Federalists' U.S. Constitution in 1789, continue today in the city's annual Fourth of July celebrations. In addition, the city's "spectacles of force," beginning with early Philadelphia's jail towers and prison walls towering over workers and citizen parks, continue today in the spectacles of paramilitary police actions on city streets and a looming criminal justice building in city center.

In a context such as this, one where the arts of public exhibition and the arts of music, performance, and parading are used by traditionally powerful groups, communities working for regenerative utopia will need to "steal the show."[2] They will need their own spectacles of liberation to reclaim urban space and refocus public perception and planning. To be sure, such spectacles should not replace the hard work of daily organizing, the patient building of movements, or the daily nurturing of communities; but neither should the creation of regenerative spectacles in the city be seen as mere ornamentation to struggles for social transformation.

We are brought back to our accounts of pilgrim spectacles of reverent, patriotic observance of the Fourth of July being challenged by the marchers' spectacles of lament over the city's plight, with their critique and hope for radical change. The marchers' challenges take on added import against the backdrop of the structures of degenerative utopia that analysts have found in Philadelphia's past and present. Those marchers, emerging from many communities of spirit, seek to direct public focus to the new structural practices they seek to deploy: resisting divisions of class and racial injustice, remembering those erased by public exhibitions and spectacles of the urban power holders, and reconnecting urban humanity to nature.

Unfortunately it is the pilgrims' structural practices and spectacles that are still given the lion's share of public attention in the United States, even when their dreaming of America yields mainly the degenerative utopia that blights the cityscapes of Philadelphia and of so many other urban sites. Cities and urban living need not be, in themselves, degenerative. They degenerate because of the structural and material practices that humans allow to dominate city life. There will be no realization of complete utopia in any of our urban spaces, but it is time, indeed, long past time, to heed the alternative practices and spectacles of such marchers—of those marching with another kind of spirit, a liberating spirit of regenerative utopia.

5
La Habana—
The City That Inhabits Me
A Multi-Sites Understanding of Location
Ada María Isasi-Díaz

"Who are the Cubans here?" The authoritarian voice belonged to
the government official who headed the project we were visiting. I
raised my hand, as did the couple that was hosting our group and
the driver of our bus. "Come with me." I got up, but our host, smil-
ing discreetly, said to me, "Not you. He means those of us who live
here." I did not feel embarrassed, but I had a sense of being
displaced, without a place to call my own. Born and raised in
La Habana, Cuba's capital, I have lived feeling that I left my heart
there, just as the song says, when I became an *exiliada* at age eight-
een. I have lived for decades thinking of the day when I will be able
to live again in Cuba. If all of this does not qualify me as a Cuban,
what does? What will?

"That is Don Luis," I said to myself. Stopping the car, I jumped out,
saying, "Don Luis, what are you doing here?" Six months earlier the

parish had thrown him a goodbye party. He was retiring and was going to do what he always said he would do, move back to Puerto Rico. "*Pues,* things did not turn out the way I expected—and here you have me, back in Rochester, New York."

———

I had just finished giving a low-key critical analysis of the U.S. economy to a friendly group. I had been asked to give the information needed to those who were gathering signatures opposing congressional plans to end the welfare laws. The third person to ask me a question said, "You speak about the U.S.A. that way because you are not an American." That night I thought to myself, how much more American can I be? I vote in general elections, in primaries and in local elections; I pay city, state, and federal taxes; I enjoy the privileges of living in New York City, I carry a U.S. passport, and my economic fate is tied to that of the United States. But she is right, I admitted to myself in the safety of my bed, in one sense I am not an American. This is not where my first loyalties lie.

———

Maggie has cut my hair for the last fifteen years. She is beginning to retire. She now works a month, then spends the next one in Puerto Rico where she is building a house. "I hope to be able to move back home for good in two years." Maggie has lived in New York City for more than twenty-five years. Yet her real home has always been her country of origin, that little island in the Caribbean that they call "the island of enchantment." Maybe I will retire to the island where I was born!

———

At the airport in La Habana, after going through the immigration checkpoint, I notice a group of uniformed persons looking over each one of us going by. Feeling somewhat uncomfortable by what I consider government surveillance—they are from the Ministry of Health—I lower my eyes and try to pass unnoticed. "*¿Se siente bien? ¿Quiere que le tome la presión?*" No, I do not want my blood pressure taken; I am feeling fine. Hearing me answer in Spanish, she says, "*¿De dónde eres?*" I am not prepared for the question. It sticks in my throat, but I finally stutter, "*Soy Americana,*" thinking that will exempt me from any tests. "*Pero, ¿dónde tú naciste?*" I tell her I was born in La Habana. Her whole attitude changes, and drawing me in with a very intimate tone, she says, "*No digas eso; tú eres cubana.*" I want to cry. She is right: I am not an American; I am a Cuban who lives in New York. I want to embrace her and kiss her and broadcast far and wide what she has said. I look at her, and holding back my tears. I say, "*Tienes razón, tienes razón!*" You are so right!

———

Lupe writes, "I am back from our yearly trip to Texas. Once we are back here in Michigan, we always say that it is too far to keep driving there. But there is something that almost forces us to go. It is as if we need to touch the land where we were born to have the strength to keep living far away from it. I don't know; maybe we are getting old and sentimental, but though right now we are saying we cannot do this again, I know we will. Maybe next time my niece can come and help us with the driving. That way we can show her all the places back there that we are always talking about. That would be so nice!"

———

I am with a group of students in the Plaza de la Revolución, posing for a picture where Fidel stands to review military parades and speak for hours. All of a sudden I see a man I know from back in the United States walking toward me. We embrace. "What are you doing here?" "I brought a group of students for an immersion experience," I reply. "And you?" "I just had to come at least for a few days. I simply could not stand any longer being away from La Habana."

———

September 11, 2001. I feel deep sadness. I am not angry; I am just sad. I am so distraught about this human race to which I belong. I am sad.

———

September 14, 2001. The Manhattan bridges are open, and I drive to work in New Jersey. Coming back, I am anxious to get to the point in the highway where I can see the city: first the Empire State Building and then, looking south, the Twin Towers. I slow down and pull to the side to take a good look. There is the Empire State. Further south: just smoke.

October 25, 2001. Today was the first time the smoke over southern Manhattan was light enough for me to see the gaping hole in the horizon where the Twin Towers used to be. Great sadness comes over me. "How could they do this to this city?" No, wait. I did not say "this city." I said "my city"!

———

*Para Ana Velford**
Lourdes Casal

Pero Nueva York no fue la ciudad de mi infancia
    But New York was not the city of my infancy
no fue aquí que adquirí las primeras certidumbres
    it was not here that I grasped truth for the first time
no está aquí el rincón de mi primera caída
    the corner where I first fell is not here
ni el silbido lacerante que marcaba las noches.
    or where I heard the piercing whistle that signaled night.
Por eso siempre permaneceré al margen,
    This is why I will always remain at the margins,
una extraña entre estas piedras,
    a stranger among these stones,
aún bajo el sol amable de este día de verano,
    even under the kind sun of this summer day,
como ya para siempre permaneceré extranjera
    just as I will always remain a foreigner
aún cuando regrese a la ciudad de mi infancia.
    even when I return to my childhood city.
Cargo esta marginalidad inmune a todos los retornos,
    I carry this marginality that is immune to all returns,
demasiado habanera para ser neoyorkina,
    too much from La Habana to be a New Yorker,
demasiado neoyorkina para ser,
    too much a New Yorker to be,
—aún volver a ser—
    —even to be again—
cualquier otra cosa.
    any other thing.

———

*This poem was originally published in a literary magazine called *Areíto* (New York) 3, no. 1 (verano 1976): 52. It was later published posthumously in *Palabras juntan revolución* (La Habana: Casa de las Américas, 1981).

Displaced or "Multi-Sites" Persons

As we move ahead into the twenty-first century, where do we turn to find elements with which to create a *proyecto histórico*—a historical project—that will move us from terrorism to biblical neighborliness, from frustration to possibilities, from unfulfilled wants to the resources we need to satisfy them? The future that we need to create to make these moves possible is indeed utopian—not utopian in the popular sense of a chimerical dream, but in the sense of being a reality that "is not but yet will be." The *mujerista proyecto histórico,* or feminist historical project, referred to here is precisely that: a utopian project that seeks to embody the preferred future of many Hispanas/Latinas living in the United States.[1] This *mujerista proyecto histórico* works as a motivator and organizing framework for our hopes for fullness of human life-liberation, which is the criterion and hermeneutical lens of all *mujerista* praxis. Our *proyecto* refers to a reality we are working to create: a concrete reality in a given place, with specific contours and content, having as its guiding principle the firm commitment that no one will be excluded.[2] The goal of our *proyecto* is to change radically, little by little, the oppressive society in which we live into a society from which no one is excluded.

When I refer to a Hispanas/Latinas *proyecto histórico,* I am talking not only about a vision of a preferred future but also about a whole spectrum of "utopian work," which in many small ways has already started: formulating utopian plans, delineating utopian processes, enabling utopian projects, creating utopian spaces and institutions. I am referring here to projects that include among their goals contributing in specific and effective ways to the material well-being of the poor, which will not happen apart from a radical change in the economic structures of most of our world. I am referring to programs and institutions that are run and administered in ways that contribute to the empowerment of Hispanas/Latinas, including us not only in their implementation but also in conceptualizing them. This means that the way society operates will include the way Hispanas/Latinas "do things," which does not obviate our cultural values and ways of understanding reality. Hispanas/Latinas' utopian projects are those that are conceptualized as ways of enabling our fullness of human life-liberation in a way that does not exclude others or is not at the expense of others.

There are many elements at play in a utopian project, in a *proyecto histórico*. Here I want to concentrate only on one, a key one: the social human person who needs to relate to others and needs to be keenly aware that we live and move and have our being within and in relation to the rest of creation, in relation to the cosmos.[3] I want to concentrate on the human person who understands herself in relation to her community and to those beyond her community, a person who needs and is creating a different world. Basing my reflection on the reality of lived experiences and understandings embedded in the stories above (and they are but a handful of a possible flood of stories), I want to talk here about the Hispanic/Latino people—particularly about Hispanas/Latinas—as "displaced" people.[4] For economic or political reasons, either as migrants or refugees, Hispanas/Latinas have had to leave our places of origin—abroad or in the United States—to look for another place to call home.[5] Little by little we learn that once we leave home we never settle down completely. Hispanas/Latinas are always on the move, creating a constant "from there to here" that results in living in many places but never fully being at home. This "from there to here" is also part of our multiple, shifting identities, a fluid social ontology[6] that is one of the constitutive elements of *mestizaje/mulatez*, the racial-ethnic-cultural-historical-religious reality that is the locus of the Hispanic/Latino community in the United States.[7]

Several clarifications are needed about using the word "displaced" in relation to Hispanas/Latinas. What shall we say about the largest group of Hispanas/Latinas, the Mexican American women who are not physically displaced, who live in the United States, the country where they were born and where their families have lived for generations? What about other Hispanas/Latinas, the second, third, and fourth generations born in the United States? All these, in my view, are displaced persons, for I am using "displaced" not as a category but as a heuristic device to describe how Hispanas/Latinas are displaced from our cultures/countries of origin as well as from what is normative in the United States.

As a heuristic device, displaced points to our permanent condition of living in the interstices of society. It reflects the condition of dissonance that we struggle to turn into a positive element in our thinking and way of acting. Otherwise we would have to submit to understandings and practices that exclude us. "Displaced" refers to the sense of not belonging that is part of our conscious selves. "Displaced" refers to what we have brought with us and hold on to, letting this richness evolve and be transformed as needed, even as we displace ourselves from our communities/countries of origin and are denied a full place in mainstream U.S. society.

Since our *proyecto* is *histórico*—material—I have chosen to use the word "displaced" as a heuristic device to point to its physical reality, to indicate that our *proyecto* is a *topos* and not a non-place. Hispanas/Latinas' *proyecto histórico* has a geographic base: we were displaced from somewhere concrete, and our "original" selves—our *first* selves as well as our *creative* selves—continue to be displaced, not only from our origins, but also from our current home (even if it is our birthplace). The preferred future we are creating is likewise to be viewed as a "space." It is turning our displaced-ness into a "multi-sites" space/place that includes both where we come from and where we are—both of which are in themselves many places that harbor spaces. We are working to create our multi-sites *proyecto histórico* here where we live, in the United States. We are also helping to create a multi-sites *proyecto histórico* in our communities and countries of origin.

What does our "displaced-ness" contribute to the creation of our Hispanas/Latinas *proyecto histórico*? I want to suggest that we bring four gifts to this utopian project—each of them subdividing into whole baskets of gifts. The first gift is the lived experience mentioned above. The community, city, country in which each of us lives is never single site: it is always a multi-sites place. This is one of the main characteristics of the twenty-first century that enriches humanity. I call it globality. Globality is not globalization, which is that ideological stance concerning modes of production and consumption that oppress and marginalize most of our world. Globality refers to the interconnectedness of all areas of our world, of all spheres of our world—ecological, animal, human—and of all the people in our world. Hispanas'/Latinas' "displaced-ness" reminds others, as well as ourselves, that economic and political isolation are impossible in today's world. To talk about ourselves as displaced persons indicates that we have to take responsibility for the consequences of our actions, for they spread out like ripples that reach every corner of a pond.[8]

The second gift we displaced people offer is our understandings and ways of thinking about life and the fullness of human life-liberation: understandings that emerge from our cultures and countries of origin. These conceptions enrich the places where we have arrived, the spaces where we hope to be safe and to fully belong. This implies, of course, that there is a multiplicity of truths that can coexist in one same physical-historical-political-social space. This is indeed possible as long as none of these truths sets itself as arbiter of the other truths. The multiple conceptions of life and fullness of human life-liberation that exist indicate this is not a static concept but a principle that can become flesh in many different ways. Our second gift, then, has to do with making this claim in the face of hegemonic understandings of "the good" prevalent in the United States. If taken seriously, our gift can help to counter the violence created by the claim that the United States is the best country in the world and that if others would only do as is done here, they will flourish.

The third gift we bring to our *proyecto histórico* is that of "dangerous memory": we must never forget where we came from.[9] Why not? I could allude here to all sorts of psychological and sociological reasons, but I will refer only to a religious one since it is the most important for me. I believe that we are not born in a given country or to a given mother and father in a haphazard way. I claim that there is a purpose for my having been born in Cuba, to my Díaz mom and my Isasi dad. And this purpose, for me, is linked to my understanding of the divine and to what is, for me, life and fullness of human life-liberation.[10] What was, what is, the purpose? As I analyze how my life has evolved, it appears to me that at least a part of it has to do with reminding the United States that this country has done harm to Cuba,[11] for example, by imposing on the original Cuban constitution an offensive and demeaning amendment that gave the U.S. government the right to invade Cuba whenever the order—as the U.S. interests saw it—was endangered.[12] Remembering and making known the oppressive and exploitative ways in which the United States has dealt with (and still deals with) our cultures and countries of origin will remind Hispanas/Latinas that our *proyecto histórico* is not a matter of our participation in oppressive structures but rather of replacing those structures with all-inclusive structures. Dangerous memories help us keep this perspective clear. Dangerous memories do not have an accusatory tone, nor do they indicate a relishing of the past for the past's sake. Dangerous memories make the past present so that we will not repeat the crimes of the past, so that we will continue to seek ways of organizing ourselves socially, economically, and politically that allow fullness of life to flourish for all.

The fourth gift that displaced Hispanas/Latinas bring is recognizing the danger of closure inherent in all utopian projects. Once a preferred future begins to unfold and to take hold *in* our reality and *of* our reality, how do we refrain from closing ourselves to other possibilities? And if we do not remain open, how can we claim that we are not excluding anyone? How do we move from the either/or that a preferred future is thought to need—for if it remains always open to change, it never becomes a concrete reality—to a both/and that affirms our choice but continues to contemplate the possibility of evolving and even radically changing as others seek to be included?[13] I believe that we displaced persons who live in the geographic-cultural interstices formed by our back-and-forth movement, we who carry constantly with us the preoccupations and dreams of those others (and those others include us as well as the people back home) who are excluded from life and fullness of human life-liberation, we are a reminder of the danger of closure. We are a reminder that closure can never be definitive and final, for we represent the excluded.

To be able to present these gifts as part of a preferred future, we Hispanas/Latinas have to ground ourselves in our own space, our own reality. Why? First of all, to ground ourselves thus helps us not to idealize our communities or countries of origin. Part of this process of idealization is, I believe, a defense mechanism against the United States' habitual undervaluing of all other nations and cultures.[14] We counter it by telling ourselves and others "tall tales" and romanticizing the places we came from. At the same time, we always need to renew our knowledge so as not to freeze in the past our communities or countries of origin. Just as we have changed in the time we have been away, our people and the culture back there have also evolved. Space and time—distance—make us long for what we have known, tricking us into thinking that the past was better than the present, and insisting that we hold on to what was.[15] As a countermeasure, we need to stay in touch with what is new in our communities/countries of origin by reinserting ourselves there as often as possible. Third, we need to realize how enticing are the privileges and benefits of U.S. society. The myth that anyone who really wants to can prosper in this country is extremely powerful— though no less of a myth because of that. Therefore, staying close to our communities and countries of origin can be an antidote to the desire to "make it" here, a needed antidote since success in the First World is always—to some degree—at the expense of Hispanas/Latinas or other Third World people. To "make it" we have to participate in present oppressive structures. Only if we stay close to our origins, only if we continue to experience ourselves as displaced, will we stand against oppressive structures and work to radically change them.

This idea of keeping in physical proximity to our communities and countries of origin is almost instinctive in the Hispanic community. Our people do everything to return home as often as possible, whether home is Cuba, Texas, or Puerto Rico. And if we fail to return alive, the community will make sure that at least we are buried back home.[16]

What are the cultural realities that hold us and, at the same time, send us forth—that inhabit us?[17] What concrete realities have been harmed, and are being harmed, by the marginalizing and exploitative attitudes prevalent in the United States toward our communities and countries of origin? How do these same attitudes affect us here in the United States? To know the reality of our sites of origin necessitates our seeing them with our own eyes and experiencing them with our own flesh.[18] For me, for example, this means returning to La Habana, analyzing La Habana. What about La Habana do I need to make present in the United States? What can I learn from La Habana that will be beneficial in the construction of our *proyecto histórico*? How will the immediacy of being in La Habana help me evade total closure? How will it help me invent ways of remaining open to future possibilities while making a firm commitment to a specific future for Hispanas/Latinas in the United States?[19]

The descriptions of places and ways of life in La Habana that follow are an attempt to give specifics regarding the meaning of being grounded in the physical reality—the geography—of one's community, one's country, of origin. These descriptions offer "outsiders" important insights into the above questions, which are essential to me as a displaced person and which provide, if not answers, at least clues. My hope as a displaced person is that readers will also appropriate at least some of what I describe, making changes as needed because of differences between La Habana and whichever place the reader calls home, but allowing my description of La Habana to challenge and expand their horizons.

La Habana—
The City That Witnessed My Birth

The sea that I was imagining more than seeing was an undefined gray mass way down there. Only slightly more than half an hour had passed since takeoff from Miami when I saw dim lights. I knew that in no time I would be landing for the first time in twenty-seven years in my homeland, in the land of my birth, infancy, and youth. I was not scared nor was I apprehensive. Indeed, what I felt was an immense desire to be back in Cuba. I had enormous expectations of reconnecting physically with my birthplace.

A huge sign with the name of the airport, the same one I had seen from the window of my departing airplane in 1960, now seemed to spell "Welcome." There was no jetway connecting the airplane to the terminal. I came down the stairs of the airplane with great intentionality, quietly but decisively claiming the right to be home regardless of the fact that the government of Cuba, even today, erects obstacles to this right. So many thoughts were crowding my mind; so many emotions were caught between my chest and my throat! I felt so much a stranger in that airport, surrounded by what seemed an inordinate number of uniformed people given the small number of travelers arriving that morning. But I also had a profound sense that I belonged there. I wanted so much to feel at home.

Volunteering to be the first in our group to face the immigration officer, I stepped up to the window. My U.S. passport shows I was born in La Habana, but he still had to ask. "Go to the end of the line so I can process the rest of the people, and then I will take care of your papers," he said. Some document I needed—who knows what!—was missing. My traveling companions, fellow seminarians, agreed to be processed and to meet me on the other side of the door. While I waited alone, leaning against the wall, I could not help feeling a bit scared, but it was mostly sadness that I felt at being required to present so much documentation, to seek permission before being able to walk the streets of my native city, La Habana, to get my passport stamped. Finally the officer called me back. I had to go to some government agency in La Habana. "You will not be allowed to leave the country if you do not have that stamp," he warned me. (When I left Cuba two weeks later, the immigration officer never looked in my passport for the stamp I had dutifully gotten that first day in La Habana.)

The moment the minibus in which we were traveling left the airport parking lot and turned left, I knew where we were: I could have driven us to La Habana! That gave me an enormous sense of relief, for I had wondered how accurate my memories were. No, I was not a stranger. I was home—and even if that sense of belonging was to be tested and even marred during my two weeks in Cuba, my time there confirmed my conviction that, though I hold American citizenship and live in New York City, I am a Cuban and the city of La Habana inhabits me.

After that first trip back to Cuba, I did not return for ten years. Then, starting in 1997, I have been able to go and actually work there every year. La Habana has changed much during these seven years, and I certainly see it through very different eyes than I did that first time I went back. What has not changed, however, is my feeling of being at home in La Habana. Regardless of the fact that I do not live there, despite the fact that I do not earn a living there and that my family does not live there, despite having to petition for an entry permit every time I go and being allowed to stay for only a month (to stay longer I have to petition and pay for an extension of my visa), despite the fact that the U.S. dollars in my pocket make my life while there different from that of the majority of Cuban people who have no access or very limited access to hard currency—despite all of this, I walk endlessly around La Habana knowing this is my city, reveling in the fact that I am more Cuban than anything else.

Aeropuerto Internacional José Martí is fifteen miles from La Habana. Often when I arrive in La Habana, instead of going north into the city, I go further south. The mother of the friend who always picks me up at the airport lives in Santiago de las Vegas, a nearby small town, and I go visit her. The people there who have to go into La Habana face one of the most difficult parts of everyday living: transportation. Before 1990, subsidies and favorable trading terms with the Soviet Union and Eastern Europe allowed a good public transportation system that linked all areas of La Habana. However, when the economic help came to an end with the unraveling of the USSR and the radical changes in governments and economic systems in Eastern Europe, gasoline—which had been rationed even before—became almost nonexistent. This, together with the lack of spare parts for buses that had been imported from the Soviet camp, brought the system of public transportation to a virtual halt. Though the system is now back on its feet, Cubans have to face long waits in the tropical heat and, when the bus finally comes, they pile in like the proverbial sardines in a can.[20]

Taxis provide another means of transportation, some of them for tourists carrying U.S. dollars and others for Cubans. The latter ones, most of them "vintage cars" from pre-1959, crowd in as many passengers as possible, picking up and dropping people along a set route. On Cuba's roads and streets, one sees every imaginable motor-driven or human-propelled contraption with wheels: bicycles—most of the time with two or even three riders—"rickshaws" for one or two persons, motorcycles with sidecars. Although less in

La Habana than elsewhere, one sees every sort of animal-pulled cart imaginable, some fitted with benches and roofs to protect against the sun. Then there is hitchhiking—*coger botella.* Everyone, young and old, women and men, tries to get a ride with anyone going by. In the main streets of La Habana, at all hours, but particularly when it is time to go to work and return home, people stand on both sides of the streets and even in the middle, between the rows of cars. One of my friends still gives rides to people in her Russian-made Lada. Another one stopped doing so after the number of people who crowded in ruined the back doors and seat of her car.

Why is it that Cubans cannot buy new cars? Of course, much has to do with the fact that what they earn, not only now but during these last forty-five years, has never been enough to allow them to save to buy a car. But there is also another reason: the government did not want some to have what others could not, the idea being to try to make everyone equal. I am not sure whether one would need special permission to buy a new car. But just to make sure this is not possible, the sales tax on a new car is 100 percent. Instead of buying new cars, therefore, Cubans keep recycling cars and constructing them from pieces salvaged from others or made from scratch. I have traveled in a car that had a pre-1959 American body, motor parts from a Russian-made Lada, and other parts salvaged from a Russian-made Moscovich. Drivers must have available on demand their sales receipts and government permits for the various parts comprising their cars. Policemen stop them randomly just to check them.

After visiting my friend's mother, I go a few miles farther south to an area where there are several military camps, to El Cacahual. I have made this a required stop for myself and those I take to Cuba. There, in an elevated spot from which one can see the whole city of La Habana, is a huge rotunda the size of a football field. It contains the tomb of Antonia Maceo, one of the heroes of Cuba's War of Independence fought against Spain starting in 1895.[21] Next to him is buried his aide-de-camp, Francisco Gómez Toro. I go there for the view of La Habana and to reminisce, for this was a site where we used to go for school outings. I go there to remember the mother of Maceo, Mariana Grajales, the Cuban "mother of the Maccabees," for history and myth tell us how she encouraged each of her sons to be willing to die for Cuba's independence.[22] However, the main reason I go there is to keep in mind that Cuban history predates 1959 and the triumph of the revolution of which Fidel (as we Cubans call Castro) was one of the leaders.

The other place I go before heading into La Habana is El Rincón. There I visit the Santuario de San Lázaro, one of the most important pilgrimage sites in Cuba. San Lázaro is the patron saint of the sick, and his feast is on December 17, when some fifty thousand devotees come to give thanks to the saint and ask for new favors. This was one of the places visited by Pope John Paul II when he came to Cuba in January 1998. The story of San Lázaro says a great deal about the relationship between the official theology and liturgy of the Catholic church and Cubans' popular religion. The latter is not church-based, definitely not church-sanctioned, and very much mixed with Santería, a Cuban version of the Lucumí religion the Yoruba slaves brought from Africa to Cuba when it was still a colony of Spain. Catholicism provides the iconography used in Santería while the Lucumí religion provides the deities. The Catholic saints are seen as incarnations or representations of the Yoruba *orishas* and provide a cover for religious practices officially banned. So San Lázaro is the *orisha* Babalú-Ayé. But this is not the only sleight of hand going on here at this Catholic church. As you approach the Santuario, you notice that the statues of San Lázaro being sold in the street are of a man on crutches and covered with sores. However, the image of San Lázaro inside the church is that of a bishop. The San Lázaro to which Cubans are devoted is the lame, sore-ridden beggar in Jesus' parable of the rich man who refused to help Lázaro, the beggar at his door.[23] In the Catholic church, saints are persons who have lived virtuous lives and are proposed to the faithful as exemplars; thus, with the liturgical reforms of the 1960s, the church removed the statues of the man in crutches from its altars. But when the people simply would not stop praying to San Lázaro, the church began to promote in Cuba another St. Lazarus, a bishop who was in its roster and whom lepers and victims of the plague in Europe had invoked centuries ago.[24]

Once we light candles to San Lázaro in thanksgiving for the good things that have come into our lives and in appeal for help with the difficult things, my friend and I are ready for the drive into La Habana. Shortly after leaving El Rincón, we see Los Cocos, Cuba's first sanatorium to house people infected with HIV/AIDS. In the early 1980s, Cuba started massive testing of its population and quarantined everyone who was HIV-positive. HIV/AIDS was seen as "a health problem/public health problem with human rights dimensions rather than a social problem/human rights problem with health repercussions."[25] By 1994, when mandatory testing was stopped, nearly all of the adult population had been tested. Mandatory confinement, from the perspective of the Cuban government, an attempt to stem the spread of AIDS and to provide the best care to those who were sick, was seen by many as a violation of human rights. Since 1993 patients can choose to live in the sanatoria— there are several others in the island besides Los Cocos—or at home. The sanatoria serve now as residences for HIV/AIDS patients as well as outpatient facilities. "Community-based education, case finding, and treatment are now being stressed." At present, "infection rates are slowly rising. . . . HIV infection among the homosexual population constitutes the fastest increase, as well as spread through prostitution. The expanding tourist industry has created new channels of spread of the virus."[26]

The road into La Habana houses numerous light industries, and it is one of the few places with commercial billboards. Almost all billboards feature slogans and quotes from Fidel encouraging people to remain faithful to the revolution. One of the students I took to Cuba decided to write down all the billboard slogans we saw, convinced that he could piece together from them a pretty accurate picture of the ideology of the government. He was right! Billboards often picture dead heroes of the revolution, particularly Che Guevara, the Argentinean doctor who fought against the dictator Batista; Camilo Cienfuegos, a popular leader who fought with Fidel and Che and who was killed in a mysterious airplane crash shortly after Fidel came to power in 1959; and Julio Antonio Mella, a student leader, one of the founders of the Cuban Communist Party, murdered in Mexico while in exile in the 1920s.

The old two-lane highway that brings us into La Habana ends at a huge fountain, now without water, that serves as a traffic circle. To the right is the old Palacio de Los Deportes, and behind it a huge sports complex with other stadiums and sport fields. Ahead of us is the Plaza de la Revolución with an imposing statue of José Martí, the father of our country, as centerpiece.[27] The tower behind the statue is the highest point in La Habana, and at present it houses a splendid museum of Martí; the top of the tower has windows from which one can see fifty miles in all directions. At the base of the statue and tower is a massive review stand and podium from which Fidel addresses the masses. I went to the Plaza in 2000, on one of Cuba's main holidays, Labor Day—celebrated on May 1—at the height of the Elián affair.[28] Though in the past the celebration consisted of military parades and Fidel's endless speeches, recently the festivities have changed. The year I was there, the atmosphere was like a party, with music and poetry readings, dances with flags, and, as always, a long speech by Fidel. That day I moved around the crowd watching intensely the faces of the people. Certainly there were some who were enthusiastically participating, but there were many who waved their Cuban paper flags and repeated slogans on cue without much ánimo—fervor. These mass gatherings are obligatory. Workers report to their jobs, children and youth to their schools, and, after attendance is taken, they are bused to the Plaza. In his speeches, Fidel instructs the people, announces policy changes and government programs, interprets national and international events, and "consults" the people, something he has done since he first entered La Habana triumphantly on January 8, 1959, days after Batista had fled. That day, during a long speech, Fidel "announced he had a question for the 'people,' thereby inaugurating a new approach to the art of governance: a dialogue with the masses, through which they would affirm his policies by chanting responses to his 'questions.' Soon he would call it 'direct democracy . . . of the marketplace,' cleaner and more honest than the old-fashioned corrupt electoral procedures of the past."[29] Undoubtedly Fidel's government by rhetoric is without precedent, and it has proven to be effective, being one of the main reasons for the staying power of his government.

As one travels around La Habana, one often sees long lines of people in front of stores waiting their turn to buy the limited goods available. The long lines have existed since the early 1960s, but they have grown longer since the beginning of the "Período Especial," the "Special Period in a Time of Peace," an unprecedented austerity plan announced by Fidel in January 1990. The government had to take strong measures in 1993 and 1994 to stop Cuba's economy from shrinking any further (between 1989 and 1993 the "economy shrunk 35 to 50 percent"[30]). One such measure was the legalization of the U.S. dollar, allowing "free markets for agricultural products and light consumer durables."[31] Despite these and other changes, feeding a family in Cuba today is a heroic deed requiring immense patience, dogged perseverance, limitless time, and a huge dose of Cuban ingenuity. I have eaten lobster at a friend's house, because the day I came to visit, someone knowing she has access to dollars came to her door selling lobster tails, though it is illegal both to fish and sell lobsters. I often have *café con leche* for breakfast, because my friends get milk from *campesinos* who either sell it illegally or buy powdered milk in the black market: milk is permissible in Cuba only for children under seven, the elderly, and people on diets because of health problems. The best bananas I have ever eaten are grown by one of my friends in her backyard where she also keeps chickens. When driving outside La Habana, I have learned to keep my eyes open for fresh cheese and garlic sold by *campesinos* who do not approach your car until they are sure you are not a government official stopping to confiscate their goods and impose a stiff fine for selling without a government permit.

I have stood in line outside a store where one has to pay with dollars to buy food to contribute to the family that was hosting me. Those in line with me—the line was needed because of the crowds—were quiet and somber, a total reversal of the loudness and lightheartedness of Cubans. I spent a long time pretending to examine merchandise on a shelf near the checkout counter so I could observe what people bought and how they paid for it. Most of them bought small quantities of food, often imported canned goods and toiletries, and they paid generally with one-dollar bills.

My friends later explained that most of these bills were tips from tourists staying at the nearby hotel or simply money the people who knew how had hustled. I have also gone with friends to the "agros"—the agricultural markets where one finds cheap produce, pork, and chicken in government-subsidized stalls, and more expensive—and better—goods at stalls where one buys directly from the campesinos and pays a higher price. Quantity and variety are not much of a problem in these markets, but obviously many Cubans cannot afford to buy there. Then how do Cubans manage to eat? Since 1962 when food rationing was begun, *la libreta*—the rationing book—has allowed each person to buy for pennies a certain amount of staple products, such as rice, beans, coffee, lard, cooking oil, household detergent, soap, and matches. But often many of these staples simply are not available or are not available in the quantity allowed, and Cubans complain constantly about the bad quality of what they get. Some items, such as cooking oil, household detergents, and soap have been missing for a long time. People get whatever is available, and then the process of exchanging what one has for what one needs begins.[32] Something still available every day is a small, very glutinous bread roll, one per person. I always smile when I eat one, remembering that the daughter of a friend of mine baptized them "*pan del Comandante*"—bread given by "*el Comandante*," as Fidel is called.[33]

That first time I went back to La Habana in 1987, after an early breakfast at the old Habana Hilton, now the Habana Libre, when the driver turned right onto Calle 23, I knew that in seconds we would be in El Malecón—a winding avenue by the sea, six lanes wide and five miles long, starting in La Habana Vieja—the old city—and ending at the Río Almendares, the river where the other municipality of metropolitan La Habana begins. El Malecón, which refers to the avenue as well as to the seawall, was designed as a jetty wall by a Cuban architect in 1857 while Cuba was still a Spanish colony, but its construction was not started until 1902, when Cuba was a U.S. military protectorate. It took fifty years to complete. The wall is about three feet high and two feet wide, providing one long continuous "*sofá*" for the delight of all. All along the wall one can see the remains of square baths hewn from the rocks, "about 12 feet square and six to eight feet deep, with rock steps for access and a couple portholes through which the waves of this tideless shore wash in and out."[34]

On the other side of the avenue, El Malecón has many faces, many personalities. The first section of the avenue borders on La Habana Vieja with its colonial buildings on one side and the very narrow entrance of La Habana's bay on the other.[35] The second zone of El Malecón starts at El Prado—a kilometer-long boulevard with a tree-lined park running down the middle—and finishes at the "Parque Maceo." This section of El Malecón, about a mile long, is called the "traditional Malecón," and it is lined with stunningly beautiful residential buildings in great disrepair.[36] This "long urban façade wall, with a continuous pedestrian arcade"[37] is now under reconstruction. The centerpiece of the park where this section ends is a huge statue of Antonio Maceo on horseback. The third part of El Malecón ends at Calle 23, in El Vedado—one of La Habana's main sectors. In this area there is a noticeable variety in the sizes and styles of the residential buildings and there are some businesses, including a European car dealership. The fourth zone starts on a rocky promontory on top of which sits the Hotel Nacional, a beautiful 1930s building with Moorish-influenced architecture. Other more modern hotels might be more attractive to tourists, but for Cubans El Hotel Nacional continues to be the "grand dame." At the foot of the small cliff is the Monumento al Maine, in honor of those who died when the American warship exploded and sank in La Habana's harbor in 1898, providing the excuse for the United States to declare war on Spain.[38] The next structure on El Malecón is a park recently constructed specifically for demonstrations against the United States, next to a modern glass structure that used to be the U.S. Embassy but is now the U.S. Interest Section. Next to this tall building are some beautiful private homes set further back from the ocean. The fifth and last zone of El Malecón starts at the Monument to Calixto García, another hero of the Cuban War of Independence. Two hotels and what used to be a private social club dominate this zone. The houses and residential buildings in this area are also set further back from the sea. The Malecón ends with a military fortress—

today it houses a restaurant—built to protect La Habana from the west in the eighteenth century. The road at this end disappears into a tunnel under the Río Almendares, coming out on the other side as a beautiful boulevard named Fifth Avenue.

The physical description anchors what El Malecón represents and the role it plays for La Habana and its residents. El Malecón has been described as the "gateway" of La Habana, and it certainly is a symbol and, in many ways, a synthesis of the city. El Malecón serves as a porch for many of La Habana's residents. Children play and ride their bikes on its wide sidewalk and leave their clothes with their parents while they bathe in the sea. This is a favorite place for lovers—young and old—and for thinkers. Fishermen try their luck here, and it is a place where one can safely discuss politics, for the sea drowns voices. The houses bordering El Malecón might have belonged to people of economic means, but *el muro del Malecón,* the wall of El Malecón, is a democratic place from which no one is excluded.[39] When I talk about La Habana as the city that inhabits me, the first image that comes to my mind is that of El Malecón, and the description that I first think of is my mother's. She went on a cruise to Panama for her honeymoon in the 1920s. The ship returned at night, and I remember my mother telling us that the lights along El Malecón were like a string of pearls around La Habana.

Being a Displaced/Multi-Sites Person

La Habana is the city that inhabits me most fully. It is not the only city that inhabits me, because as a displaced person, I am a multi-sites person. However, La Habana is undoubtedly the city that provides most of the resources for my "imaginary," for my gaze into the present and the future, and a main point of reference in how I position myself in relation to the past.[40] Going to La Habana is a way of refurbishing—renovating, renewing, revamping—my resources for day-to-day living (*lo cotidiano*). Though as a multi-sites person I do not belong fully in La Habana, the ways I do feel at home in La Habana renew my desire to make the United States, where I spend most of my time, a place I can also call home. Being in La Habana gives me new impetus for the struggle (*la lucha*) to create a *mujerista proyecto histórico* where La Habana as well as the United States will be home for me. Having walked the streets of the city where I was born and grew up, I return to New York more sure of who I am, less foreign to myself. Many parts of me that in the United States mark me as foreign, make me in Cuba simply "part of the bunch." The centering or grounding that being in La Habana gives me in many ways makes me a better U.S. citizen, for I return here with a renewed vigor for life, for my work, and for the multiple commitments that mark my life.

Every time I go to La Habana I go with preoccupations and questions that emerge, as they always do, from what is happening in my life, from my interpretation of world events, from my commitment to issues of justice, from my dedication to those I love. Returning from La Habana I have new questions and new insights into my questions. I have new preoccupations that I do not leave behind but instead add to my *cotidiano* in the many other sites where I live as a displaced person. For example, one of the last times I was in La Habana I began to see the importance of paying attention to globality and globalization, to learn what they mean, how they operate, and how they affect our present communities.

What made me turn my attention to these phenomena is the fact that in La Habana, contrary to most places in the world, globality does not work very well. To start with, telephone communications even within Cuba are limited since many people still do not have telephones. Calls to any place outside Cuba are expensive and, with rare exceptions, one cannot dial an international call from telephones in private homes. Those who can have a second telephone with a special line allowed by the government.[41] Moreover, the postal system simply does not work. The most common experience is for letters not to arrive—either coming or going— and if they arrive, the news certainly will not be fresh. Use of the Internet is severely limited. The number of people with computers is extremely small, and Internet access must be authorized by the government. News from Cuba and abroad is limited to what is provided on official television channels, radio stations, and newspapers. The physical insularity of Cuba is replicated at all levels of contact and communication with the rest of the world. In many ways, Cuba does stop at the wall of El Malecón.

Cuba's lack of communication with the rest of the world is a result of its political and economic isolation, partially self-imposed, partially imposed by U.S. policies. Its insularity is broken by people who visit Cuba,[42] those who leave legally or illegally,[43] and those who live outside the island and keep in touch with relatives and friends, sending them medicine and money to the tune of a billion dollars a year.[44] Through these kinds of contacts, Cuba becomes part of globalization, a "global economic matrix" that encompasses not only the production and distribution of goods but also "a worldwide system of governance and power."[45] In us and through us who live outside but are indeed part of Cuba, our island interacts with the world in unofficial ways. Unfortunately, much of the interaction is not positive for, though some Cubans and Cuban Americans benefit from globalization, a great number of us Cubans who live outside the island—the majority—belong to the middle and working classes and are the ones used and abused by globalization.

Being used and abused is the reality not only for the majority of Cubans but also, of course, for all Hispanic/Latinos in the United States. Therefore, it is important—as we, Hispanas/Latinas, create our preferred future, as we work on our *proyecto histórico*—to pay attention to the role globalization plays in our oppression. The fact is that globalization creates a "demand for lower-paid workers," a category that covers most Hispanas/Latinas. The "global cities" that are the key links in the network of globalization are "most often supported . . . by large populations of immigrant workers who perform the blue-collar, industrial, low-wage, dirty work of the global economy as the valets, the coffee-stand servers, the janitors."[46] In the "global cities," such as New York, London, Frankfurt, Bangkok, Santiago (Chile), and a few others, global capital is not the only element present. There is also a workforce made up of "women, immigrants, people of color"[47] without which these cities could not perform the highly specialized transactions that are intrinsic to globalization. This makes these cities attractive to job-seekers. In other words, "some of the infrastructure that enables globalization enables and indeed may induce migration."[48]

Though much has been said about globalization in relation to capital, little or no attention has been paid to the "transnationalization of labor" it requires. The "global cities" need the support of labor coming from communities such as ours: the Hispana/Latina communities. These communities, instead of the cities and the countries in which they live, provide the principal source of identification to these workers, most of them being displaced/multi-sites people. Given that these "global cities" are sites not only for global capital but also for a "global workforce," they also contribute to "the formation of transnational identities."[49] The global cities are characterized not only by "their telecommunication infrastructure and international firms, but also . . . [by] the many different cultural environments they contain. . . . An immense array of cultures from around the world, each rooted in a particular country, town, or village, now are reterritorialized in a few single places, places such as New York, Los Angeles, Paris, London, and most recently Tokyo."[50]

These global cities, therefore, have the effect of "unbundling" the territoriality of nations, for they relate among themselves and depend on each other much more than they relate to other cities in their same nation or to the nation in which they are located.[51] This unbundling of territoriality also leads to the "unbundling of sovereignty." "We are seeing the relocation of various components of sovereignty onto supranational, nongovernmental, or private institutions."[52] And because the working class that supports globalization in New York, for example, has much more in common with those who support globalization in, let's say São Paulo, Brazil, than with the elite population of New York, "new notions of community, of membership, and of entitlement" are emerging, linking workers across national boundaries.

Another element generated by globalization, an unintended element that nonetheless plays a significant role in the way transnational labor continues to relate to the people "back home," is that of family remittances. We Cubans are not the only ones to send monies back to our country of origin. Hispanas/Latinas as a whole practice this "philanthropy of the poor,"[53] which often is the main sustenance of our families and friends back home. The need for family remittances are to a large extent a consequence of globalization.

> As the global north has put increasing pressures on governments in the global south to open their economies to foreign firms, these countries have become poorer even as certain sectors within them have gotten very rich. Government and large sectors of the population in many of these countries have come to depend more and more on the remittances of immigrants in the global north, which overall are estimated at an annual 70 billion dollars over each of the last few years.[54]

This sort of sharing and deployment of resources also takes place in Hispanic/Latino families born in the United States. Though I have never seen statistics, I am sure that such monies are economically important to the local communities, particularly if we come from small towns. The fact is, then, that the poor of the world are maintaining the poor of the world. The poor of the world in the United States are maintaining families and friends back home as well as contributing in a significant way to the economies and governments of our communities and countries of origin.

These mechanisms of globalization, at work in many cities with great concentrations of Hispanas/Latinas, have created new ways, meanings, and understandings of the back-and-forth characteristic of displaced/multi-sites people. Globalization is not only about transnational economic spaces; it is also about transnational people, and that is what many of us Hispanas/Latinas are. Definitely, globalization is exploitative, benefiting only 20 percent of the world population. However, if we look carefully at the mechanisms of globalization, I propose that we can use some of the unintentional side effects of globalization in constructing our *mujerista proyecto histórico.*

First, as these global cities of the globalization network concentrate larger and larger numbers of Hispanas/Latinas (and of course also Hispanic/Latino men), we begin to be a critical mass that can organize to pressure the government for our rights and the benefits we have earned by being productive members of this society. This will be useful for the *mujerista proyecto histórico* only if we are clear that our goals are to create a society from which no one is excluded, and not to participate in oppressive structures. Second, with the growing dependence of Third World governments and U.S. town, city, and state governments on remittances from those of us who work outside their parameters, can we not turn our generosity into influence? Can we not find effective ways of using the economic leverage that remittances give us to reverse the structural adjustment programs imposed on governments by the World Bank and the International Monetary Fund that have cut health, education, and other social programs? Third, the transnational labor force of globalization of which Hispanas/Latinas are a part contributes a basis for identity that makes clear we have to see ourselves in relation to our communities and countries of origin. We have much more in common with women in our communities and countries of origin than we have with the privileged women of the global cities. Being conscious of this and finding effective means of maintaining close contact with each other can aid our struggle to create a *proyecto histórico* from which no one is excluded.

La Habana, the city that inhabits me, is the city that challenges me, the city that makes me ask new questions, the city where I dream dreams and see visions. La Habana is the city that is home— but not completely, for La Habana also displaces me, sending me forth to be a multi-sites woman. La Habana is one of the key organizing principles in my life: who I am and who I want to be, what I want to do with my life—a life that will always have to honor the discontinuities and ruptures created in me and for me. La Habana is the place that precludes me from returning; it fragments me, but this fragmentation is not problematic to me. Rather, it facilitates the interstices through which I can reach our *mujerista* utopian project, or where I can stand free of the objectifying gaze of those who insist on constructing me as "other."[55] La Habana has its all-encompassing effect on me as I walk its streets, manage its heat or its surprising coldness (having fallen prey to the propaganda that in-January-it-is-hot-in-the-tropics), and maneuver through its still somewhat unfamiliar systems in order to get food, find transportation, make a phone call, or buy an airline ticket. La Habana, with its sad buildings holding on to a splendor that shines through crumbling walls, imposes itself in irrevocable beauty on my heart and mind and soul:

this is the city, the place, the locality, the human geography that was and continues to be my starting point as a displaced/multi-sites person committed to a *mujerista proyecto histórico* that will exclude no one. La Habana: "*Si no existieras yo te inventaría, mi ciudad de La Habana.*"[56]

Notes

Preface

1. See Saskia Sassen, *Globalization and Its Discontents: Essays on the New Mobility of People and Money* (New York: New Press, 1998).

2. Michel Foucault, "Of Other Spaces," trans. J. Miskowiec, *Diacritics* 16 (1986): 22.

3. John Berger, *The Look of Things* (New York: Viking, 1974), 40, cited in Edward W. Soja, *Postmodern Geographies: The Reassertion of Space in Critical Social Theory* (New York: Verso, 1989), 22, 61.

4. Henri Lefebvre, "Reflections on the Politics of Space," trans. M. Enders, *Antipode* 8 (1976), 31, cited in Soja, *Postmodern Geographies*, 80.

1. Taking the Train

1. See Kevin Starr, *Embattled Dreams: California in War and Peace, 1940–1950* (Oxford: Oxford University Press, 2002).

2. Mike Davis, *City of Quartz: Excavating the Future in Los Angeles* (London: Verso, 1990).

3. Fredric Jameson, *Postmodernism, or, The Cultural Logic of Late Capitalism* (Durham: Duke University Press, 1991).

4. See H. Paul Santmire, *The Travail of Nature: The Ambiguous Ecological Promise of Christian Theology* (Philadelphia: Fortress Press, 1985).

5. See Sallie McFague, *The Body of God: An Ecological Theology* (Minneapolis: Fortress Press, 1993).

2. A Theologian in the Factory

1. For two examples of essays in political theology in the United States from theologians of the dominant or privileged racial communities, see John A. Coleman, *An American Strategic Theology* (New York: Paulist Press, 1982), and Dennis P. McCann and Charles R. Strain, *Polity and Praxis: A Program for American Practical Theology* (Minneapolis: Winston Press, 1985). McCann and Strain misunderstand Lonergan on at least two counts. First, they mistakenly assume that in the scheme of functional specialization, Lonergan has located political theologies at the level of communications. Nothing could be further from the truth. In response to questions raised in his course on "Method in Theology" (Boston College, fall 1979), Lonergan maintained that the theologies emerging from an empirical notion of culture are responsible to all the functional specialties. The theologian cannot communicate appropriately what she or he has not researched historically and dialectically interpreted. For Lonergan, communications is not some "vaguely defined afterthought" (McCann and Strain, *Polity and Praxis*, 18). Rather, this last functional specialization is of enormous importance, requiring that the converted theologian select a medium or means of communication adequate and appropriately nuanced for the audience or audiences in specific cultural and social contexts. Second, in discussing Matthew Lamb's heuristic use of Lonergan's methodology, McCann and Strain reveal not only a misunderstanding of Lamb and his enterprise, but of Lonergan's transcendental imperatives (ibid., 44). First, the transcendental imperatives regard an orientation in the human person—and, yes, even the oppressed and marginated person, the person of the "Third World," the "wretched of the earth." The transcendental notions regard the human capacity "for seeking and, when found, for recognizing instances of the intelligible, the true, the real, the good" (Bernard Lonergan, *Method in Theology* [New York: Herder and Herder, 1972], 282). The transcendental precepts are rooted in the dynamism of human consciousness and intentionality; they are invariant over cultural change. They are transcultural—but are made specific in human knowing, decision, and action. What Lamb suggests is that "Lonergan's dialectic analysis takes a critically grounded stand on the transformative values" generated in the exercise of the transcendental imperatives (Matthew L. Lamb, *Solidarity with Victims: Toward a Theology of Social Transformation* [New York: Crossroad, 1982], 138). McCann and Strain quite rightly locate the burden of Lamb's orthopraxis in what he means by "the heuristic of discerning values and disvalues" (Lamb, *Solidarity with Victims,* 137; McCann and Strain, *Polity and Praxis,* 44). But they seem unaware of just what Lamb means by that heuristic

and its import. For what that heuristic is, is cognitional theory; and it is integrally related to the praxis McCann and Strain so vigorously advocate. For if our knowing is inattentive, uncritical, careless, and irresponsible, we are likely to bend or justify our knowing to what we already are doing. We are likely to adjust our theory to our current practice, rather than allowing our noetic reflection to open the range of choices and possibilities for probable solution. We open ourselves to the probability of the ideological justification of our practice.

2. Such histories would counter the dominant theories of historiography, which have treated the indigenous North American peoples, enslaved Africans, Mexicans, and peoples of Asian descent merely as foils and antagonists in Anglo- and Euro-American accounts. For one counterexample, see Francis Jennings, *The Invasion of America: Indians, Colonialism, and the Cant of Conquest* (Chapel Hill: Institute of Early American History and Culture/University of North Carolina Press, 1975).

3. With the structure of the human good, Lonergan offers a field theory by which the theologian might apprehend, understand, judge, evaluate, and explain comprehensively the social and cultural matrix. At the same time, the structure cannot be simply detached from the philosophy of action compactly located in the cognitive and moral effort to answer the questions, What am I doing when I am knowing? Why is doing that knowing? What do I know when I do it? What is my practical, intelligent response to what I know or what am I to do? What values are realized in my decision and choices?

4. See Ze'ev Chafets, "The Tragedy of Detroit," *The New York Times Magazine,* July 29, 1990, 20–26, 38, 42, 50–51.

5. Certainly it provides an obvious but not altogether superficial link to the concerns of Catholic Social Teaching. In *Rerum Novarum*, Leo XIII denounced the exploitation and destitution of industrial workers at the end of the nineteenth century. The pope judged the condition of workers and the masses of poor laboring children, women, and men as inhuman. Moreover, he criticized the control of production and the concentration of wealth as an impetus to greed. He urged that the rich give to the poor, that laborers be paid just wages, and that trade associations or unions be recognized. Finally, he emphasized private property as a natural right and an essential ingredient in the stabilization of a society.

These concerns were repeated in 1931 by Pius XI in the encyclical *Quadragesimo Anno* (The Reconstruction of the Social Order), which commemorated the fortieth anniversary of *Rerum Novarum*. This encyclical was written during a time of grave worldwide economic and political upheaval. Indeed, Franklin Delano Roosevelt celebrated the encyclical, calling it "just as radical as I am" and "one of the greatest documents of modern times," and quoted from it during a major campaign speech in Detroit on October 2, 1932 [Quoted in David Milton, *The Politics of U.S. Labor: From the Great Depression to the New Deal* (New York and London: Monthly Review Press, 1982), 123].

Pius XI encouraged the organization of unions to protect the rights of the laborer; he argued that increased social wealth ought to be distributed among individuals and classes for the common good, that workers ought to be paid a wage sufficient to support the worker and the worker's family; and asserted that opportunity for work should be provided to all those willing and able to work. Finally, the pope criticized the abuses of capitalism and socialism and called for the moral renovation of society coupled with action for justice based on love.

6. True not only of Detroit, but of the emergence of the global factory.

7. See *North-South: A Programme for Survival: Report of the Independent Commission on International Development Issues,* ed. Willy Brandt (Cambridge: MIT Press, 1980), and *Common Crisis North-South: Cooperation for World Recovery* (Cambridge: MIT Press, 1983).

8. Tissa Balasuriya, *The Eucharist and Human Liberation* (Maryknoll: Orbis, 1979), 49.

9. Dieter Hessel, *Social Ministry* (Philadelphia: Westminster, 1982), 53. The notion of overdevelopment was first discussed by the social theorist and ethicist Louis-Joseph Lebret, in *The Last Revolution* (New York: Sheed and Ward, 1965). Lebret's work has been made more accessible to readers in Denis Goulet, *A New Moral Order: Development Ethics and Liberation Theology* (Maryknoll: Orbis, 1974).

10. See Richard J. Barnet and Ronald E. Müller, *Global Reach: The Power of the Multinational Corporation* (New York: Simon and Schuster, 1974).

11. John Rawls, *A Theory of Justice* (Cambridge: Harvard Belknap Press, 1971).

12. Alan B. During, "Ending Poverty," in *State of the World 1990* (Washington, D.C.: Worldwatch Institute, 1990), 137–38.

13. Hessel, *Social Ministry,* 53.

14. Ibid., 100–101.

15. During, "Ending Poverty," 148.

16. Edmund Wilson, *American Earthquake* (Garden City, N.Y.: Doubleday, 1958), 232, quoted in Robert E. Conot, *American Odyssey,* (New York: Morrow, 1974), xxviii.

17. Conot, *American Odyssey,* xxviii.

18. B. J. Widick, *Detroit: City of Race and Class Violence,* rev. ed.(Detroit: Wayne State University Press, 1989), xvii.

19. Lynda Ann Ewen, *Corporate Power and Urban Crisis in Detroit* (Princeton: Princeton University Press, 1978).

20. Melvin G. Holli, *Detroit,* Documentary History of American Cities Series (New York: Franklin Watts, 1976), 1.

21. Ibid., 3.

22. Ibid.

23. Ibid., 6.

24. Ibid., xv.

25. Ibid., xiv; *cf.* Conot, *American Odyssey,* 122.

26. Conot, *American Odyssey,* 130.

27. Ibid., 131.

28. Holli, *Detroit,* xv–xvi.

29. Ibid., xv.

30. Ibid.

31. Ralph J. Bunche, *The Political Status of the Negro in the Age of FDR,* ed. Dewey W. Grantham (Chicago: University of Chicago Press, 1973), 587, quoted in August Meier and Elliott Rudwick, *Black Detroit and the Rise of the UAW* (Oxford and New York: Oxford University Press, 1979), 16.

32. Holli, *Detroit,* xvi.

33. Dan Georgakas and Marvin Surkin, *Detroit: I Do Mind Dying: A Study in Urban Revolution* (New York: St. Martin's Press, 1975), 32.

34. Ibid., 40. Given the tendency to "overlook" black women (focusing either on black males or white females), it would be important to find out the percentage of black female workers—and whether they were counted among black males or white females.

35. Following the outbreak of the Detroit rebellion on July 29, 1967, President Lyndon Johnson issued Executive Order 11365, which established the National Advisory Commission on Civil Disorders. Chaired by Otto Kerner, governor of Illinois, the commission included leaders in business and government, two members of the House and Senate, the president of the AFL-CIO, and the executive director of the NAACP. The president pledged the commission the full support and cooperation of the federal government; but by the fall of 1967, the president's time and the energy of the government were absorbed by the Vietnam War. Robert Conot, who served as a special consultant to the commission, writes: "The President had believed the riots to be organized, and when the commission—working in conjunction with the FBI—discovered they had been unorganized and spontaneous, he lost interest in the work of the commission" (Conot, *American Odyssey,* xxvii). The *Kerner Report* issued on March 1, 1968, raised more questions than it could answer. Most of all it overlooked the fact that the conditions it studied were interrelated genetically, socially (politically, economically, technologically), and culturally one with another.

36. See *Kerner Report,* 35–200.

37. Matthew Lamb makes the point that this orientation of the good of order toward human liberty and interpersonal relations is overlooked in Michael Novak's "false presentation of Lonergan's understanding of the human good" ("The Social and Political Dimensions of Lonergan's Theology," in *The Desires of the Human Heart: An Introduction to the Theology of Bernard Lonergan,* ed. Vernon Gregson [New York: Paulist, 1988], 281). See Novak, *The Spirit of Democratic Capitalism* (New York: Simon and Schuster, 1982), 71–80. Novak writes that "the systems through which the ordinary goods of daily life are brought to us are themselves goods of order" (*Spirit of Democratic Capitalism,* 77).

38. Lonergan, "Lectures on Topics in Education," 34. This is the transcript of unpublished lectures given at an institute on education sponsored by Xavier University, Cincinnati, Ohio, August 3–14, 1959. I am working from a typescript transcribed and edited by John Quinn.

39. Conot, *American Odyssey,* 161–62.

40. Ibid., 162.

41. Ibid., 176.

42. Ibid.

43. Ibid.

44. Ibid., 164.

45. Ibid., 175.

46. Ibid., 156–58; *cf.* Meier and Rudwick, *Black Detroit,* 13.

47. Daniel Bell, *The Coming of the Post-Industrial Society* (New York: Basic, 1973), 129–42; *cf..* Barnet and Müller, *Global Reach,* 326–27.

48. Richard J. Barnet, *The Lean Years: Politics in the Age of Scarcity* (New York: Simon and Schuster, 1980), 245.

49. Ibid.

50. Georgakas and Surkin, *I Do Mind Dying,* 34.

51. Ibid., 35.

52. Ibid., 35, 37.

53. Ibid., 105.

54. Ibid., 102.

55. Ibid.

56. Ibid., 104.

57. Ibid.

58. Ibid., 109–10.

59. Ibid., 101.

60. Ibid., 103–4.

61. Barnet and Müller, *Global Reach,* 323.

62. Ibid.

63. Ibid.

64. Ibid., 325.

65. Ibid.

66. Ibid.

67. Ibid., 328.

68. For a compelling and sensitive treatment of the concerns of members of the working class for freedom and dignity, see Richard Sennet and Jonathan Cobb, *The Hidden Injuries of Class* (New York: Random House, 1973).

69. Barnet and Müller, *Global Reach,* 328.

70. Ibid., 328–33.

71. James Boggs, *The American Revolution: Pages from a Negro Worker's Notebook* (New York and London: Monthly Review Press, 1963), 90. While Boggs repeatedly uses the phrase "creative imagination," it is clear that although he

offers no explicit cognitional or epistemological proposals, he advocates serious questioning, critical thinking, and analysis—not only of the political and economic and factory situation, but also of our *own* thinking about the situation. Such reflection to promote thorough and critical understanding precedes evaluation and effective social praxis.

72. This view contests that of Edward Banfield, *The Unheavenly City* (Boston: Little, Brown, 1970). Banfield insists that workers (the lower classes) are unable to live beyond the moment, unable to think so as to provide for the future in creative and imaginative and intelligent ways.

73. Lamb, "Social and Political Dimensions of Lonergan's Theology," in *Desires of the Human Heart*, 278.

74. Lonergan, *Insight: A Study of Human Understanding* (1959; New York: Philosophical Library, 1970), 622–27.

75. William P. Loewe, "Dialectics of Sin: Lonergan's *Insight* and the Critical Theory of Max Horkheimer," *Anglican Theological Review* 61, no. 2 (April 1979): 235.

76. Lonergan, *Insight*, 741.

77. Ibid., 721, 723, 699.

78. Robert Franklin of Emory University, Atlanta, Georgia, has identified "rap," quite correctly, I think, as the discourse of the underclass. This music provocatively uncovers the despair, the anger, the raw rage, the feelings of utter hopelessness of so many members of the African American community. At the same time, it reveals their surrender to the surd of living in the United States under late twentieth-century capitalism.

79. See *The Church with AIDS: Renewal in the Midst of Crisis*, ed. Letty M. Russell (Louisville: Westminster John Knox, 1990).

3. Tasting the Bitter with the Sweet

1. This "most dangerous city" blow came in 1997 from a survey taken by *Money* magazine drawing upon 1995 FBI crime statistics.

2. By 1873 some Italian immigrants began choosing New Jersey, whereas previously they had emigrated primarily to New York. Thus Newark became one of the first U.S. cities with a large Italian immigrant community. By the turn of the century, it ranked fifth in the nation, behind New York, Philadelphia, Chicago, and Boston. The best-known segment of this community lived in Newark's "Old First Ward." For an extensive treatment of the Ward before urban renewal, see Michael Immerso, *Newark's Little Italy: The Vanished First Ward* (New Brunswick: Rutgers University Press and Newark Public Library, 1997). For case histories and neighborhood descriptions of various ethnic groups in New Jersey, including Italians, compiled between 1939 and 1941, see *America, The Dream of My Life: Selections from the Federal Writers' Project's New Jersey Ethnic Survey*, ed. Davis Steven Cohen (New Brunswick: Rutgers University Press, 1990).

3. This is as of the 1990 U.S. Census—which also ranked New Jersey fifth in total number of foreign-born persons and fourth in proportion of foreign-born. The state also ranks high in total diversity, whereas states like California are becoming more concentrated around one or two nationalities. See *Keys to Successful Immigration: Implications of the New Jersey Experience*, ed. Thomas J. Espenshade (Washington, D.C.: Urban Institute Press, 1997); especially chapter 1, "New Jersey in Comparative Perspective," by Espenshade.

4. The institutions are Rutgers University–Newark, Seton Hall Law School, the University of Medicine and Dentistry of New Jersey, Essex County College, and the New Jersey Institute of Technology. At one time home to over a thousand industries, Newark is credited with helping to start the Industrial Revolution. Later, many of Thomas Edison's ventures began in Newark. I am indebted to Charles F. Cummings, Newark city historian and assistant director of the Newark Public Library in charge of special collections, for detailing many positive aspects of Newark, both historical and current, as well as for insights regarding its small size and tax base.

5. It passes through Newark, Bloomfield, Glen Ridge, Montclair, Verona, Caldwell, and West Caldwell. Caldwell produced the state's only native-born president, Grover Cleveland.

6. For an amusing autobiographical account of Jersey City, growing up there, and enduring its reputation, see Helene Stapinski, *Five-Finger Discount: A Crooked Family History* (New York: Random House, 2001).

7. I am indebted to Elizabeth Del Tufo, longtime resident of the ward and former executive director of the Newark Boys Chorus, for her reflections. Even though the schools have not improved and many have moved away, she said, she has chosen to remain because of such things as recently improved maintenance of the park, easy shopping, and sidewalks. (Telephone interview with the author, January 7, 2002.)

8. Imperiale won an at-large city council seat in 1969, and in 1971 accomplished the unheard-of by winning a state assembly seat as an independent. In 1973 he won election as an independent to the state senate. Although in 1974 he lost a close race to Kenneth Gibson, who became the first African American mayor of a major eastern U.S. city, Imperiale did receive 43.7 percent of the vote. And while he was also defeated in 1977 for reelection to the state senate, in 1979 he ran again and won as a Republican. In 1981 Imperiale won another term to the state assembly, this time as a Republican, and in 1984 was a delegate to the Republican National Convention. After that, his career took a downturn as he lost several bids for county and national office. He died of complications related to kidney failure in 1999 at the age of sixty-eight.

9. Although some theatrical license is taken with its physical placement along Tony's drive, this cathedral is prominently although briefly featured in the regular opening sequence of the HBO television series *The Sopranos*. Actual scenes along Bloomfield Avenue have also appeared during the show's several seasons.

10. It is well known that Italians did not "fit neatly into the American Catholic church. Italian Catholicism clashed with the austere practices of the dominant Irish. Italians placed greater emphasis on the intercession of the saints, and they mixed formal religion with ancient beliefs in a world of good and evil spirits." Douglas V. Shaw, *Immigration and Ethnicity in New Jersey History* (Trenton: New Jersey Historical Commission, 1994), 43. As a child, given my experience of the church and popular culture such as film, I assumed that all priests had Irish names.

4. Degenerative Utopia in Philadelphia

1. Laura Rigal, *The American Manufactory: Art, Labor and the World of Things in the Early Republic* (Princeton: Princeton University Press, 1998), 21–22.

2. Ibid., citing among others Thomas Doeflinger, *A Vigorous Spirit of Enterprise: Merchants and Economic Development in Revolutionary Philadelphia* (Chapel Hill, N.C.: University of North Carolina Press, 1986).

3. Jerome I. Hodos, "Globalization, Regionalism and Urban Structuring: The Case of Philadelphia," *Urban Affairs Review* 37.3 (January 2002): 358–79.

4. For a critique of Abu-Jamal's trial, see Amnesty International, *The Case of Mumia Abu-Jamal: A Life in the Balance* (New York: Seven Stories Press, 2000). For the most recent, thorough examination of the case to date, see Dave Lindorff, *Killing Time: An Investigation Into the Case of Mumia Abu-Jamal* (Monroe, Mass.: Common Courage Press, 2002).

5. John Anderson, *Burning Down the House: MOVE and the Tragedy of Philadelphia* (New York: Norton, 1987), the collectively authored *20 Years on the Move* (Philadelphia: MOVE Organization, 1991), and Margot Harry, *"Attention MOVE! This Is America!"* (Chicago: Banner Press, 1987).

6. See Russell Thornton, *American Indian Holocaust and Survival: A Population History since 1492* (Norman: University of Oklahoma Press, 1987), 70; John E. Pumphrel, "Foreword," in *William Penn's Own Account of the Lenni Lenape or Delaware Indians,* ed. Albert Cook Myers, tercentenary ed. (Wilmington, Del.: Middle Atlantic Press, 1970), 7.

7. This attitude is clearly documented in Mary Maples Dunn and Richard S. Dunn, "The Founding, 1681–1701," in *Philadelphia: A 300-Year History,* ed. Russell F. Weigley (New York: Norton, 1982), 5–6.

8. Samuel Bass Warner, *The Private City: Philadelphia in Three Periods of Its Growth* (Philadelphia: University of Pennsylvania Press, 1968), xi.

9. Ibid., 65.

10. Ibid., 49–51.

11. See Carolyn Adams, David Bartelt, David Elesh, Ira Goldstein, Nancy Kleniewski, William Yancey, *Philadelphia: Neighborhoods, Division, and Conflict in a Postindustrial City* (Philadelphia: Temple University Press, 1991), 12.

12. Warner, *Private City,* 50.

13. Ibid., 223.

14. On the decay of the manufacturing city, see William Julius Wilson, *When Work Disappears: The World of the New Urban Poor* (New York: Knopf, 1996), 29; Adams et al., *Philadelphia*, 25–27, 175–81.

15. Mark Alan Hughes, *Poverty in the Cities* (Washington, D.C.: National League of Cities, 1989). Cited in Adams et al., *Philadelphia*, 27.

16. Harry A. Bailey, Jr., "Poverty, Politics and Administration: The Philadelphia Experience," in *Black Politics in Philadelphia*, ed. Miriam Erskowitz and Joseph Zikmund II (New York: Basic, 1973), 173.

17. Adams et al., *Philadelphia*, 48–49.

18. Buzz Bissinger, *Prayer for the City* (New York: Vintage, 1997), 372, citing the *Philadelphia Daily News*, March 21, 1997.

19. Ibid., 33–34.

20. N. R. Peirce and C. W. Johnson, "Reinventing the Region: The Peirce Report," *Philadelphia Inquirer*, March 26, 1995, H1–H12.

21. For one view on this period, from an organizer who now sits on Pennsylvania's death row as a result of a trial that was a travesty of justice, see Mumia Abu-Jamal, *Live from Death Row* (Reading, Mass.: Addison-Wesley, 1995). On the bogus trial that has many now calling for Abu-Jamal's immediate release, see Amnesty International, *The Case of Mumia Abu-Jamal*.

22. Joseph R. Daughen and Peter Binzen, *The Cop Who Would Be King: Mayor Frank Rizzo* (Boston: Little, Brown, 1977).

23. Ibid., 150–51.

24. For more extensive treatment of this notion of utopics, see Louis Marin, *Utopics: Spatial Play*, trans. Robert A. Vollrath (Atlantic Highlands, N.J.: Humanities Press, 1984).

25. David Harvey, *Spaces of Hope* (Berkeley: University of California Press, 2000), 156.

26. Ibid., 156–57.

27. On Marx and utopianism, see Nicholas Lash, *Matter of Hope: A Theologian's Reflections on the Thought of Karl Marx* (Notre Dame, Ind.: University of Notre Dame Press, 1982).

28. Nan Ellin, *Postmodern Urbanism* (London: Basil Blackwell, 1996).

29. *Heterotopia: Postmodern Utopia and the Body Politic,* ed. Tobin Siebers (Ann Arbor: University of Michigan Press, 1994), 24–28.

30. Graham Ward, *Cities of God* (New York: Routledge, 2000), 42.

31. Ibid. 75–77.

32. Paul Tillich, "The Technical City as Symbol," in Paul Tillich, *The Spiritual Situation in Our Technical Society,* ed. J. Mark Thomas (Macon, Ga.: Mercer University Press, 1988), 179–80.

33. See Saskia Sassen, *Cities in a World Economy* (Thousand Oaks, Calif.: Pine Forge/Sage Press, 1994).

34. Tillich, "Technical City," 183.

35. Ibid.

36. Marin, *Utopics*.

37. See my more explicitly Christian theological works: Mark Taylor, *Remembering Esperanza: A Cultural-Political Theology for North American Praxis* (Maryknoll: Orbis, 1990); and *The Executed God: The Way of the Cross through Lockdown America* (Minneapolis: Fortress Press, 2001).

38. Adrienne Siegel, ed., *Philadelphia: A Chronological and Documentary History, 1615–1970* (Dobbs Ferry, N.Y.: Oceana Publications, 1975), 1.

39. On this rendering of habitus, see anthropologist Nancy Scheper-Hughes, *Death without Weeping: The Violence of Everyday Life in Brazil* (Berkeley: University of California Press, 1992), 184–85. Bourdieu himself locates the best explanation of this notion in Pierre Bourdieu and L. Wacquant, *Invitation to Reflexive Sociology* (Cambridge: Polity Press, 1992). See also Pierre Bourdieu, "Habitus," introducing a volume that reflects on his notion in relation to urban environments, in Jean Miller and Emma Rooksby, *Habitus: A Sense of Place* (Burlington, Vt.: Ashgate, 2002), 27–34.

40. Rigal, *American Manufactory,* 13, emphasis added.

41. Ibid., 29–34.

42. Ibid., 42.

43. Ibid., 33.

44. Warner, *Private City,* 233.

45. Bissinger, *Prayer for the City,* 371.

46. Rigal, *American Manufactory,* 185.

47. Linda K. Kerber, *Women of the Republic: Intellect and Ideology in Revolutionary America* (Chapel Hill: University of North Carolina Press, 1980), 73.

48. Bruce Laurie, "Fire Companies and Gangs in Southwark: the 1840s," in *The Peoples of Philadelphia: A History of Ethnic Groups and Lower-Class Life, 1790–1940,* ed. Allen F. Davis & Mark H. Haller (Philadelphia: University of Pennsylvania Press, 1973), 72.

49. Barbara Clark Smith, "Food Rioters and the American Revolution," *William and Mary Quarterly*, 3rd series, 51, no. 5 (1994). For more on women in the early republic, see Mary Beth Norton, *Liberty's Daughters: The Revolutionary Experience of American Women, 1750–1800* (Boston: Little, Brown, 1980), Ray Raphael, *A People's History of the American Revolution* (New York: New Press, 2001), 107–44, and Howard Zinn, "The Intimately Oppressed," in *A People's History of the United States* (New York: Harper & Row, 2000), 103–24.

50. On the history of this culture of resistance that the Federalists' "American Revolution" repressed, see "A Motley Crew in the American Revolution," in Peter Linebaugh and Marcus Rediker, *The Many-Headed Hydra: Sailors, Slaves, Commoners and the Hidden History of the Revolutionary Atlantic* (Boston: Beacon Press, 2000), 211–47.

51. See the portrait *Pat Lyon at the Forge* in Rigal, *American Manufactory,* 180.

52. Benjamin Rush, "Observations on the Procession," cited in Rigal, *American Manufactory,* 36.

53. Ibid., 37.

54. Allen B. Ballard, *One More Day's Journey: The Story of a Family and a People* (New York: McGraw-Hill, 1984), 18–20.

55. Ibid., 19.

56. E. Digby Baltzell, *The Philadelphia Gentlemen: The Making of a National Upper Class* (Philadelphia: University of Pennsylvania Press, 1958), 239–41.

57. Ballard, *One More Day's Journey*, 18.

58. John K. Alexander, "A Year . . . Famed in the Annals of History," in *Philadelphia: 1776–2076: A Three Hundred Year View*, ed. Dennis Clark (Port Washington, N.Y.: Kennikat, 1975), 18. Alexander is a professor in the history department, University of Cincinnati.

59. Ballard, *One More Day's Journey*, 78.

60. Charles Pete T. Banner-Haley, *To Do Good and To Do Well: Middle-Class Blacks and the Depression, Philadelphia, 1929–1941* (New York: Garland, 1993), 43.

61. Rigal, *American Manufactory*, 146.

62. Ibid., 149, 159.

63. From *The Papers of Thomas Jefferson*, cited by Rigal, *American Manufactory*, 151 and 235 n. 9.

64. Rigal, *American Manufactory*, 150.

65. Ibid., 163, citing Wilson's commentary in *American Ornithology*.

66. For one account of all these processes as part of a settler community's vision and practice toward Indian peoples, see David Stannard, *American Holocaust: The Conquest of the New World* (New York: Oxford University Press, 1991).

67. Rigal, *American Manufactory*, 21.

68. Ibid., 16.

69. See Hodos, " Globalization," 364.

70. Cindy Hing-Yuk Wong and Gary W. McDonogh, "The Mediated Metropolis: Anthropological Issues in Cities and Mass Communication," in *American Anthropologist* 103.3 (March 2001): 96–111, esp. 105.

71. Ibid., 106.

72. Rigal, *American Manufactory*, 199.

73. Ibid., 199, emphasis added.

74. For a discussion of this portrait, see ibid., 179–96.

75. "Trampling the Public Trust: Philadelphia Police Abuses Reveal Systemic Injustice," *Action Update*, October 1995 (Hyattsville, Md.: Equal Justice USA, 1995), 3–5.

76. Tina Rosenberg, "The Deadliest D.A.: Philadelphia's Lynne Abraham," *New York Times Magazine,* cover story, July 16, 1995, 20–25.

77. See "The Bombing of West Philly," *Frontline* public television series, narrated by Judy Woodruff, produced by South/Fanning, directed by Smith/McFadden (Corporation for Public Broadcasting, May 5, 1987).

78. John Edgar Wideman, *Philadelphia Fire* (New York: Henry Holt, 1990), 19.

79. Ibid. 159.

80. Ibid. 12–16.

81. For the three degenerative dynamics of the American manufactory in Philadelphia, see above, pages 82–91.

82. On "stealing the show" in Christian communities, see Mark Lewis Taylor, "Stealing the Show: The Way of the Cross as Dramatic Action," in Taylor, *The Executed God*, 99–126.

5. La Habana—The City That Inhabits Me

1. *Mujerista* theology is a Latinas' liberation theology that has as its source the religious understandings and practices of Latinas living in the United States.

2. *Una sociedad donde quepan todos,* "a society in which everyone fits," is a leitmotiv of the Zapatistas in Chiapas, southern Mexico, and pointedly expresses the goal of their struggle.

3. I thank Carlos Sintado for pointing out the need to articulate this understanding.

4. I certainly do not consider my reflections applicable only to the Hispanic/Latino community living in the United States. However, this is the community I have as my point of reference and as my context and to whom I am accountable, particularly Hispanas/Latinas.

5. There is a difference, of course, between the categories of migrants and refugees, but here I include all of us under the rubric "displaced persons."

6. Catherine Keller, "Seeking and Sucking—On Relation and Essence in Feminist Theology," in *Horizons in Feminist Theology—Identity, Tradition, and Norms,* ed. Rebecca S. Chopp and Sheila Greeve Davaney (Minneapolis: Fortress Press, 1997), 55.

7. See Ada María Isasi-Díaz, "A New *Mestizaje/Mulatez*: Re-conceptualizing Difference" in *A Dream Unfinished—Theological Reflections on America from the Margins,* ed. Eleazar S. Fernandez and Fernando F. Segovia (Maryknoll: Orbis, 2001), 203–19. A different but no less important analysis is that of Manuel Mejido, "The Fundamental Problematic of U.S. Hispanic Theology," in *New Horizons in U.S. Hispanic Latino(a) Theology,* ed. Benjamín Valentín (New York: Pilgrim Press, 2003).

8. I heard Franz Hinkelammert make a distinction between globality and globalization years back at a meeting in Germany. Born in Germany, Hinkelammert is an economist who for the last forty years has lived first in Chile and then in Costa Rica. He is a part of the Department of Investigation in San Jose, Costa Rica. Though the distinction I make here between globality and globalization is based on what Hinkelammert said, the elaboration I present is my own.

9. Johann Baptist Metz, *Faith in History and Society* (New York: Seabury Press, 1980), 184. This phrase is used extensively. I refer to Metz because this is where I first saw it used years ago.

10. There is a sentence in a prayer to Jesus that I have said for the last forty-three years that captures what I am saying here in a succinct way. Referring to Cuba, it says, *"Tú nos la diste y por eso es para nosotras un legado sagrado"*—You gave it to us and that is why it is for us a sacred legacy.

11. I am not ignoring the fact that Cubans have also done enormous harm to our country. My point here is that we have to contribute to building a preferred future that is "situated" in the United States and, therefore, I am pointing out what needs to change in the United States. I realize fully that there is much also that needs to change in the communities and countries of origin of Hispanas/Latinas.

12. The U.S. government asked the members of the Cuban constitutional assembly to write this into our constitution. When they refused to do so, even if Cuba was at the time under U.S. military rule, it was imposed by the U.S. government as an amendment to our constitution. Franklin Delano Roosevelt abrogated this amendment in 1934. Marifeli Pérez-Stable, *The Cuban Revolution: Origins, Course, and Legacy* (New York: Oxford University Press, 1999), 4, 7.

A military occupation of Cuba lasted from 1906 to 1909. Marines were landed in 1910 to protect U.S. interests and citizens, and in 1917 to persuade Cuba to enter World War I. To protect U.S. properties, the marines remained in Cuba until 1923. Tad Szulc, *Fidel: A Critical Portrait* (New York: Morrow, 1986), 96.

13. See David Harvey, *Spaces of Hope* (Berkeley: University of California Press, 2000), 182–96.

14. The view prevalent in this society is that the United States is the best country in the world and that everyone else should follow its example.

15. Nowhere is this idea expressed better or more beautifully than in the first *copla*—couplet—of the elegy Jorge Manrique, the fifteenth-century Spanish poet, wrote on the death of his father. See Jorge Manrique, *Obras Completas*, 2nd ed., edición y prólogo de Augusto Cortina (Buenos Aires: Espasa Calpe, 1942), 135.

16. A few years ago there was a wave of murders in New York City, the victims being taxi drivers from the Dominican Republic. In each and every case the community raised funds to send their bodies back to the Dominican Republic for burial. Cubans living in the United States have asked to be cremated when they die so their ashes can be taken back to Cuba as soon as possible. The ashes of many have already been returned to the island. Most of them have been taken by relatives in their handbags; a few have been returned through the expensive official process that has been set up. Undoubtedly, many Latinas and Latinos do not wish to return to their community or country of origin and are happy to die and be buried in the land to which they have moved. However, I think statistics uphold the claim that Latinas have a very high rate of visiting our communities/countries of origin and taking our dead back to be buried there. Will this be different in the future? It remains to be

seen, of course, but the fact that there is a continuous flow of people from our countries of origin coming into our communities in the United States will, I believe, keep fresh our links to where we came from.

17. I borrow this phrase, and the title of this chapter, from the title of the book by Magali García Ramis, *La ciudad que me habita,* 2nd ed. (Río Piedras, PR: Ediciones Huracán, 1997).

18. I realize that returning to or visiting one's country of origin might not be possible for some Hispanas/Latinas or Latinos, or that some might simply choose not to return. Those who cannot, for whatever reason, may still fit into the schema I present here, I believe. Those who choose to return might very well exclude themselves from the schema presented here.

19. Though many Cubans living in the United States would disagree with me, maybe even the majority, I continue to believe that we all have something to learn from today's La Habana, from how it deals with space, from its radically different way of organizing its socio-political-economic structures—radically different from the way they are organized in the United States—and from the struggles of the Cuban people there.

20. Cuban inventiveness is legendary, and how effective we are in dealing with crisis is seen everywhere in La Habana when a *camello*—camel—comes into sight. This is a bus made by adding bodies to two articulated flatbed Mack trucks. The place where the bus "articulates" dips lower than the bodies. This camel-like feature accounts for its name. *Camellos* weigh twenty tons, adding terrible wear and tear to the streets of La Habana. They cost about $30,000 and carry 220 persons, though usually no fewer than 300 cram in. Those who travel by *camellos* know that they are not very safe. It is not uncommon to have wallets and other items lifted, and women always complain of being molested physically and verbally. Much of this kind of information I have gathered during the years I have been going to Cuba. See Christopher P. Baker, *Havana Handbook,* Moon Travel Handbooks (Emeryville, Calif.: Avalon Travel, 2000). Of all the travel guidebooks, I find the "hermeneutical lens" of this one to be the most balanced, and I have yet to catch a single mistake in the information it provides!

21. Since the time of his death, Maceo has been called *"El Titán de Bronce"*— The Bronze Titan—a reference to the fact that he was black and to his military acumen. As a young man, he led troops in the first Cuban war for independence, called the Ten Years War. He refused to accept the armistice that brought that armed conflict to an end because the Spaniards would not abolish slavery nor give Cuba its independence. His renewal of the armed struggle at that time is known as *La Protesta de Baraguá*—the Protest of Baragua—the place where Maceo met with the Spanish general to discuss his demands. In three months, however, Maceo had to abandon his efforts. Refusing to surrender, he left Cuba (so allowed by the Spanish general) while his followers accepted the armistice Maceo had refused to embrace. (Since 1990 Fidel has used *La Protesta de*

Baraguá in his speeches—it can be seen in La Habana's billboards—to indicate his refusal to give in and bring about political and economic reforms in Cuba.) In the 1895 Cuban War of Independence, Maceo was the insurgents' army's second in command. Bypassing La Habana, he was able to bring the fight for independence to the western part of the island. He was killed in battle, together with his assistant, on December 7, 1896.

22. Her parents had come from the Dominican Republic and settled in Santiago de Cuba, in the eastern part of the island, where she was born June 26, 1808. With her first husband she had four sons. After she died—though contemporary research indicates maybe they divorced—she married Marcos Maceo, who was a Venezuelan. With him she had five sons, nine sons in all. It is said that when her husband died fighting in the first Cuban war for independence, she cried out to the youngest of her sons, then a little boy, "Stand up tall; it is already time that you should fight for your country." She herself took to the battlefield, to help whichever way she could. On November 23, 1893, less than two years before the start of the Cuban War of Independence, Mariana Grajales Cuello died in Jamaica. Thirty years later her remains were taken to Cuba and buried in the Cemetery of Sta. Ifigenia, in her birth city of Santiago. See Raúl Ramos, "Mariana Grajales," available at http://www.ain.cubaweb.cu/mujer/mariana.htm (accessed August 25, 2002); María Elena Balán, "Mariana Grajales, madre mayor de Cuba," available at http://www.nnc.cubaweb.cu/historia/historia27.htm (accessed August 25, 2002); J.A. Sierra, "The Timetable. History of Cuba. The Antonio Maceo Timeline," available at http://www.historyofcuba.com/history/mactime1.htm (accessed August 25, 2002).

23 See Luke 16:19-31.

24 This may very well be the Lazarus of the Gospels, brother of Martha and Mary, whom Jesus raised from the dead. A derivation of his name, *lazaretto,* is given to places where lepers are cared for. This move by the church not only removed a nonhistorical character from the roster of the saints but also attempted to distance San Lázaro from Babalú-Ayé, who is represented in Africa as an old man with a wooden leg. Jorge Castellanos and Isabel Castellanos, *Cultura Afrocubana 3—Las Religiones y Las Lenguas* (Miami: Ediciones Universales, 1992), 57–59.

25. Tim Holtz, MD, MPH, "Summary of Issue of HIV-AIDS in Cuba—APHA Cuba Tour, August 1997;" available from http://www.cubasolidarity.net (accessed September 1, 2002).

26. Ibid.

27. Born in 1853 in La Habana, José Martí was the soul of the Cuban War of Independence, advocating equality for all Cubans and the establishment of democratic processes. He worked in the United States to bring together all the factions of Cuban exiles and fundraised to finance the war. He landed in Cuba with a few others, and gathering supporters along the way, he was finally able

to link with Antonio Maceo and his army, but died in battle shortly thereafter, on May 19, 1895. Martí's copious writings have been the inspiration of every single struggle for freedom in Cuba. He was also a poet and is one of the key figures of Latin American literature.

28. On November 22, 1999, Elizabeth Brotón illegally left Cuba for the United States in a sixteen-foot motorboat with her son, Elián González. The boat capsized the next day, and Elizabeth and Elián survived by hanging on to inner tubes. On November 25 two of the other survivors came ashore and Elián was rescued at sea near Ft. Lauderdale. His mother had died. The next day Elián was entrusted to his great-uncle who lives in Miami. On November 27, Elián's father in Cuba demanded his return. The U.S. Immigration and Naturalization Service decided that the father in Cuba had the right to custody; the attorney general upheld this decision. Elián's Miami family did everything possible to keep the six-year-old child: they applied for political asylum for him, applied for temporary custody, and filed suit in federal court to challenge the INS ruling. Elián became a battleground between the Cuban government and the large and politically powerful anti–Cuban government Cuban community in Miami. The federal government in the U.S. never wavered in its decision regarding the right of the father to custody. His father was granted a visa and came to Washington, D.C. After months of public demonstrations in Cuba and Miami, legal procedures, and meetings with Elián's family in Miami by well-known community and national leaders trying to find a solution, on April 22, 2000, federal agents stormed the Miami house of Elián's family and took him to his father, then in Washington, D.C. On June 28, after the U.S. Supreme Court refused to block his departure, Elián returned to Cuba. The political machinations at work in this case are many. What is often lost is that the González family is an example of the terrible divisions that exist in Cuban families. The grandfather of Elián and his family are sympathizers with the Castro regime. His brothers who exiled themselves in Miami are not. Elián became embroiled in the painful divisions that had split the family years before. The day I was at the Plaza de la Revolución, Fidel placed a phone call from the podium to Elián's father, who already had the child with him in Washington. After the ceremonies at the Plaza, Fidel led the people in a march of several kilometers to the staging area that had been recently built outside the U.S. Interest Section in La Habana. Here demonstrations took place almost daily during the early months of 2000 with children being brought from school and workers from their workplaces to participate. For a full chronology of the events, see "Elián González Chronology," available from http://www.washingtonpost.com/wp-srv/nation/sidebars/elian_timeline.htm (accessed September 2, 2002).

29. Szulc, *Fidel*, 469.

30. Pérez-Stable, *Cuban Revolution*, 174.

31. Ibid., 176–77.

32. Food subsidies are one of the reasons Cubans had been able to live with such small salaries. Since staples are now not always available, Cubans' monthly salaries are said to allow people to live for two weeks. The rest of the time, those who have dollars manage, while the rest have to rely on their creative resourcefulness or simply have to be hungry. Workers and students do receive free meals but, again, the quality is so terrible that many simply do not eat them.

33. Fidel holds the rank of major in Cuba's armed forces. The rank of general was created for his brother Raúl who heads the Ministry of the Interior, controlling the army and the security apparatus of the government.

34. Baker, *Havana Handbook*, 108.

35. This part of El Malecón is called Avenida del Puerto, and it is not considered to be officially part of El Malecón. However, the seawall continues in this area, and many of us consider it to be part of El Malecón. In my description, I am following the division of El Malecón used by a course taught at Harvard Design School in Cambridge, Massachusetts. See Lelan Cott, Instructor, "1511: Havana, Cuba III: El Malecón," Harvard Design School—Spring 2002 Courses," available from http://courses.gsd.harvard.edu/2002/spring/1511 .html (accessed September 2, 2002).

36. Though a few of the buildings have been torn down for safety reasons, many of them still stand with the help of scaffolds, which Cubans refer to as "crutches." When I look at those old buildings, I always have the sense that they are standing against all odds to show us the honor and grace inherent in the act of surviving.

37. Cott, "1511: Havana, Cuba III," 2.

38. The eagle that was on top of two forty-foot-tall columns was toppled in 1961 by an angry mob on the occasion of the United States–sponsored invasion by Cubans aiming to overthrow Fidel's government, the invasion known as the Bay of Pigs.

39. Jorge Mañach, "El Muro del Malecón," in *Estampas de San Cristóbal* (I) (Cuenca, España: Editorial Trópico, 1995).

40. Stuart Hall, "Cultural Identity and Diaspora," in *Colonial Discourse and Post-Colonial Theory: A Reader,* ed. Patrick Williams and Laura Chrisman (New York: Columbia University Press, 1994), 392–403.

I am using here "the imaginary" as a noun. This usage as a noun is quite extensive in contemporary Spanish writings—*el imaginario*—and it refers to the "inventory" of ideas, images, symbols, that exist or are possible to imagine or conceive by a group of people or a person.

41. In La Habana I stay with a friend who has a telephone, and just outside her house, on the sidewalk, there are two public telephones from which I can make long-distance calls using cards bought at kiosks of ETECSA, the Cuban telephone company (a partnership with an Italian company). Last year I went to the sidewalk to call the United States and found that the phones were bro-

ken; the children from across the street play with them. So I started to walk, trying to find another phone. I finally found three phones about ten blocks away. One was broken and the other two were being used. I waited. After ten minutes the woman using the phone allowed me to make my call before she made her next call. Gratefully I dialed, but it took me a full five minutes of constant dialing to get a line and have my call go through. I ran back to the house, for my host was waiting for me. As I tried desperately to make my legs go faster, I started to laugh, remembering that when I went to China for a women's meeting a few years ago, I found a telephone on top of the Great Wall. The friend with me thought it would be wonderful to call her daughter in Geneva from the Great Wall. So she picked up the phone and, using her Swiss credit card, soon reached her daughter, having had to dial only once! My friend lives in Cuba.

42. The Cuban government indicated that in 2001, 120,000 Cubans and Cuban Americans traveled to Cuba. The money spent by those who travel to Cuba, plus the remittances sent to the island from abroad, provide 14 percent of the hard currency available to the Castro government. Pablo Alfonso, "Castro necesita más dólares del exilio," available at http://futurodecuba.org /Castro%20Necesita%20Mas%20Dolares%20del%20Exilio_htm (accessed August 25, 2002).

43. The lowest estimate of those who have left Cuba illegally in boats and rafts since 1959 is 78,000 (personal e-mail from Holly Ackerman, August 28, 2002). See Holly Ackerman and Juan M. Clark, *The Cuban Balseros: Voyage of Uncertainty* (Miami: Policy Center of the Cuban American Council, 1995). No fewer than one-fourth of them have perished. This number does not include those who left by boat with permission of the Cuban government in 1965 through Camarioca (5,083) and in 1980 through Mariel (120,800). See Cuban-American Military Council, "Support for a Democratic Transition in Cuba (excerpts)," available from camcocuba.org/news/lyndon.html (accessed September 1, 2002); and U.S. Coast Guard Office of Law Enforcement, "Mariel Boatlift," available from www.uscg.mil/hq/g-o/g-opl/mle/mariel.htm (accessed September 1, 2002). Besides the estimate of 78,000 leaving by boat, there is no estimate of the Cubans who have deserted: those who were allowed to leave Cuba to visit families or to go to different events—whether representing Cuba officially or on their own—have not returned.

44. Exact figures are impossible to obtain. The best estimate is that Cubans send to the island between 830 million and 1 billion U.S. dollars. Oscar Espinosa Chepe, "El estado real de la economía cubana," *Cuba en Transición* 10 (2000), 15. Seemingly, three years later, a much higher amount is being sent to Cuba by those of us living outside the island. "A government economist . . . says that remittances from Cuban Americans topped $1 billion last year" ("The dollarised revolution," *The Economist* [August 2, 2003]: 37).

The remittances have to be sent through third countries and now there is a way of sending money through the Internet for those with a credit card. See "International Money Transfer" at www.international-money-transfer -consumer-guide.info (accessed June 8, 2004).

The government in Cuba indicates that approximately 62 percent of Cubans have access to dollars. These are not only the ones who receive money from abroad but also a small number of Cubans who work in key industries such as construction and oil and receive stimulus in U.S. dollars. It also includes those who work in tourism. (See Pablo Alfonso, "Castro").

45. This understanding of globalization is Saskia Sassen's—see her *Globalization and Its Discontents: Essays on the New Mobility of People and Money* (New York: New Press, 1998). Here I am quoting from Charlotte Snow, "Saskia Sassen calls for a democratic approach to globalization's impact," in *University of Chicago Magazine;* available at http://magazine.uchicago.edu/9812 /html /invest2.htm (accessed June 8, 2004).

46. Ibid.

47. Saskia Sassen, "The Global City: Strategic Site/New Frontier" available at http://www.india-seminar.com/2001/503/503%20saskia%20sassen.htm (accessed June 8, 2004).

48. Ibid.

49. Saskia Sassen, *Globalization and Its Discontents*, xxx. Though Sassen does not apply her theory to workers from less economically advantaged areas within the United States, I do. I believe that Mexican American and U.S.–born Hispanas/Latinas are indeed part of this transnational labor pool to which Sassen refers.

50. Ibid., xxx–xxxi.

51. Ibid., 24–25, and many other places throughout the book.

52. Ibid., 92.

53. This use of "philanthropy" was shared with me by Yolanda Tarango, to whom I am grateful for conversations that contributed to several points in this chapter. She heard it from Barbara Ehrenreich in an interview about her book, *Nickeled and Dimed—On (Not) Getting By in America* (New York: Holt, 2001).

54. Sassen, "The Global City."

55. Gayatri Chakravorty Spivak, "'Questions of Multiculturalism,' interview by Sneja Gunew (August 30, 1986)," in *The Post-Colonial Critic: Interviews, Strategies, Dialogues,* ed. Sarah Harasym (New York: Routledge, 1990), 66.

56. "If you did not exist I would invent you, my city of La Habana." Closing verse of a poem by Cuban poet Fayad Jamis.